THE
ROBERT R. CARKHUFF
PRODUCTIVE
TEACHER 2

—An Introduction to Instruction—

with

Cheryl B. Aspy, Ed.D., and David N. Aspy, Ed.D.
International Consortium for Productivity in Education

David H. Berenson, Ph.D.
Tallahassee, Florida, Public Schools

Terry Bergeson, Ph.D.
Washington Education Association

Karen Garr, M.A.
Raleigh, North Carolina, County Public Schools

Andrew H. Griffin, Ed.D.
Georgia Association of Education

Human
Resource
Development
Press

Copyright© 1984 by
Human Resource Development Press, Inc.
22 Amherst Rd.
Amherst, Massachusetts 01002 (413) 253-3488

Bernice R. Carkhuff, Publisher

First Edition, First printing, May, 1984

Library of Congress Cataloging in Publication Data
International Standard Book Number 0-914234-78-1

Cover Art by Donald Gates
Cover Design by Tom Bellucci
Composition by The Magazine Group
Printing and Binding by Heffernan Press

About the Authors

Robert R. Carkhuff, Ph.D., is Chair, Carkhuff Institute of Human Technology. Among the most-cited social scientists of the twentieth century, he is author of three of the 10 most-referenced social science texts, including his two-volume masterpiece, *Helping and Human Relations.*

Cheryl B. Aspy, Ed.D., is Co-Director for Research and Development, International Consortium for Productivity in Education, Amherst, Massachusetts. A math teacher by training, she is co-editor of *Third Century in American Education.*

David N. Aspy, Ed.D., is Director, International Consortium for Productivity in Education. A former science teacher and coach, he is author of *KIDS Don't Learn from People They Don't Like* and *The Best and the Brightest—The Master Teacher in the Age of Information.*

David H. Berenson, Ph.D., is Assistant Superintendent for Administration, Tallahassee, Florida, Public Schools. A former science teacher, he is co-author of *The Skills of Teaching* series.

Terry Bergeson, Ph.D., is Vice President, Washington Education Association, Tacoma. An English teacher, counselor and coach, she continues to train teachers in teaching and leadership skills.

Karen Garr, M.A., is an elementary teacher, Raleigh, North Carolina, County Public Schools. A former chairperson, Women's Caucus, National Education Association, she is President of the largest education association in North Carolina.

Andrew H. Griffin, Ed.D., is Associate Executive, Georgia Association of Educators. A social science teacher by training, he is a co-author of *The Skilled Teacher* and *The LEAST Method of Discipline.* Throughout his professional career, Dr. Griffin has emphasized teacher training in teaching and learning skills in a multicultural and community-based context.

Preface to the Teacher

"The future of a nation may be found in the minds and skills of its children. The vision of the future may be found in the minds and skills of their teachers."

Human and information resources have already displaced capital and natural resources as the sources of growth in economic productivity. Economists now project that human and information resources, alone and in interaction with each other, will account for 75% of productivity growth. Thus, human resource development, along with advancements in knowledge, become the critical ingredients in the Age of Information.

The source of human and information resource development is education and training. Economists now project that education and training will account for 75% of human and information resource development. Thus, education becomes the critical source of productivity growth.

The primary source of effective education and training is teaching skills. While pre-instructional learner variables account for most of the variability in learning achievement, effective teachers have an extraordinary effect upon achievement. Trained and skilled teachers have more than a 95% chance of achieving any learning skills objectives.

The skills of effective teachers may be divided into two potent factors: 1) those having to do with preparing the content; 2) those having to do with delivering the content to the learners. Effectively trained with these skills, teachers have nearly a 100% probability of achieving any reasonable learning objective.

Volume I is "An Introduction to Curriculum Development." Volume II is "An Introduction to Instruction." Properly practiced and programmatically applied, these teaching skills will enable the teachers to make their full contribution to human and information growth and development and, thus, productivity growth in the Age of Information.

Washington, D.C.   RRC
May, 1984

ROLLING
On Being Alive

I am rolling, rolling, rolling
I see the earth
I see the sky
I am rolling, rolling, rolling.

When I was three
I loved the earth and sky
I loved others and myself
As only innocence could love.

When I was six
I loved the earth and sky
I loved others and myself
As others love to love.

When I was twelve
I liked the earth and sky
I liked others and myself
Sometimes!—and under certain circumstances.

When I was twenty-four
I could no longer love the earth and sky
I could no longer love others or myself
I could no longer love at all.

Then a child, however old
Took me by the hand and said,
"See the earth, See the sky"
And through his eyes I saw again.

Finally, I am me once more
I love the earth and sky
I love the others as myself
As only the courageous can love.

I am rolling, rolling, rolling
I see the earth
I see the sky
I am rolling, rolling, rolling.

—Robert R. Carkhuff—

Table of Contents

I.
INTRODUCTION
AND OVERVIEW

The teaching and learning processes involve the contributions of both teachers and learners. The teachers
use their teaching skills to facilitate the learners' movements through the learning process. The chapters are
organized around the principles of learning as follows:

> **Chapter 1—Learning in the Age of Information**
> All productive learning involves the
> naturalistic patterns found in experien-
> tial exploration, personalized under-
> standing, and behavioral action.
> **Chapter 2—Planning for Learning Management**
> All productive delivery plans em-
> phasize learner management.

Facilitating the learning process is the essential task of
making a teaching delivery.

1.
Learning in the Age of Information

Perhaps the greatest changes in the Age of Information are in the individuals themselves. Basically, most people were prepared for an earlier age. Even the most advanced and futuristic find themselves unprepared for the effects of the expanding press of information. They have no guidelines to follow, no mentors to advise them and no data to predict for them. Nowhere is this seen more clearly, than in the shift from the earlier dictum, "Work harder!", to the new dictum, "Work smarter!" The great source of productivity in the Age of Information is human processing or thinking (Aspy, Aspy and Roebuck, 1984; Carkhuff, 1984).
In turn, the key to human processing is learning. To be sure, the Age of Information may be seen as an Age of Learning. We are constantly processing new information and we are constantly learning new ways to process new information.

An Analysis of Individuals

Again, we may view the changing components, functions and processes during the changing eras (See Table 1-1). As can be seen, the components of an individual emphasize his or her physical, emotional and intellectual makeup. During the Industrial Era, humans were seen physically as mechanical appendages to machinery. More recently, during the Hardware Age, humans have come to be seen as machines themselves. Now, during the Age of Information, we begin to view humans as humans, with the distinguishing human characteristic being the 100 billion neurons each of us has in our brains. Indeed, we view humans in the terms of our latest, "state-of-the-art" machinery. We even describe our brain components in our latest scientific language: "Each neuron is programmed in chemical and electronic languages." To be sure, we now search to emulate the human condition by viewing machines as humans, i.e. having the potential to think or process in human-like ways.

In our emotional development, humans have moved in one generation from emotional dependency (Industrial Era) through independency (Electronics Era) to a recognized need for interdependency in the Information Age. Interdependency emphasizes the dependency of each of us upon all of us. With constantly changing data bases, no one can control the information. Indeed, those closest to the phenomenon are most familiar with information relating to it. Thus, policy-makers depend upon managers who depend upon supervisors who depend upon the delivery personnel. Interdependency is seen best in the teaching-learning process where each, in turn, is teacher of the other and learner from the other.

Table 1-1 Individual Dimensions in the Different Eras

INDIVIDUALS

DIMENSIONS	OLD (Industrial Era)	TRANSITION (Electronics)	NEW (Information Age)
COMPONENTS Physical Emotional Motivational Interpersonal Intellectual	"Man as Mechanical Appendage" Dependent Incentives Top-Down Technologies	"Man as Machine" Independent Achievement Lateral Systems	"Humans as Processors" Interdepent Actualization Bottom-Up Models
FUNCTIONS Living Learning Working	Orderly Living Linear Thinking Corporate Obedience	Participative Living Systems Thinking Corporate Identification	Creative Living Human Processing Entrepreneurial Initiative
PROCESSES Explore Understand Act	Stimulus No Understanding Response	Explore Experience Understand Goals Act Upon Programs	Analyze Dimensions Operationalize Objectives Technologies Programs

In speaking of human motivation, the changes are similar. No longer do people work exclusively for external incentives as they did in the Industrial Age. People once worked to satisfy their need to achieve or their pride in craftsmanship. Now they work to actualize their resources in more and more productive efforts.

In their interpersonal relationships people used to employ "top-down" patterns. The boss operated from a "Give and Go" base: the superior *gives* the order and the subordinate *goes* out and performs the task. With transitional attention to lateral or peer relationships, people are now learning to operate from the "bottom-up": each person *gets* and *gives* images, *merges* the images in the task to be performed and *goes* out and does his or her part to complete the task. Thus, interpersonal relations in the Information Age define the interdependency of that age.

Intellectually, the individual's substance or specialty skills have changed in emphasis. During the Industrial Era, the individual developed simple, step-by-step linear technologies. During the Electronic Age, the individual realized the need for systems that integrate a number of variables at one time. Now in the Age of Information, the individual needs to be able to develop inclusive and operational models of substance in multidimensional space.

The individual functions may be summarized in living, learning and working functioning. As can be seen, the Industrial Era emphasized orderly, top-down, "by-the-numbers" dependent relationships. In turn, the Electronics Era emphasized participative democracy in which children, students and employees alike participated in designing goals for their own destinies. Now, the Information Age requires creative living: each individual is responsible for processing the entire data base and for making his or her own unique contributions to the social good.

Learning emphasizes the greatest difference between ages or eras. During the Industrial Age, the emphasis was upon linear thinking: making specific, step-by-step responses to specific, dimension-by-dimension stimuli. Indeed, schools were dominated by the memorization of linear responses and this memorization was conceived of as the cornerstone of education. During the Electronics Era, individuals received training in systems thinking: the relating of variables and their interactions in time and space. To be sure, the great electronics breakthroughs like digital and telecommunications technologies were a product of the systems planning that coordinated these variables. The Age of Information requires human processing that produces multidimensional models that are quantitatively and qualitatively superior to the responses that stimulus materials were calculated to elicit, i.e. every response builds upon a creative integration of all previous responses.

The emphasis upon working functions shifts from corporate obedience in the Industrial Era through corporate identification in the Electronics Era to entrepreneurial initiative in the Information Age. Entrepreneurial initiative involves each individual at each performance station processing to improve their own individual performance as well as the unit's or organization's productivity.

Individual processing emphasizes exploring, understanding and acting. Exploring emphasizes the experiential relationship of individuals with stimulus experiences: *individuals explore where they are in relation to the experience.* Understanding emphasizes the cognitive relationship of individuals with their response goals: *individuals understand where they are in relation to where they want or need to be with their experiences.* Acting emphasizes the behavioral relationship of individuals to their response program: *individuals act to get from where they are to where they want to be.*

During the Industrial Era, individuals were conditioned to make simple, straightforward responses to the stimuli. There was no need to understand their relationship with the goals for responding. They simply learned and implemented habitual, non-thinking action responses.

During the Electronics Era, individuals participated in the processing of stimuli. They participated in exploring their experience in relation to the stimuli. They participated in understanding their relationships with their goals. They participated in selecting preferred courses of action to achieve their goals. They participated in acting upon their programs to achieve their goals.

Finally, during the Information Age, individuals are proferred the entire data base with which to engage in more productive cognitive processing: exploring and analyzing the dimensions of an experience or task; understanding and defining the objectives for the experience or task; developing and implementing the technological action programs to achieve the objectives. The demands are for increasingly sophisticated learning strategies and programs.

Entry into the Age of Information increasingly requires cognitive changes. These changes call for us to learn the cognitive processing skills required to process the daily changing data we receive (Carkhuff, 1984a, 1984b). They require that we understand the learning processes we seek to facilitate in others in order to become productive teachers in the Age of Information.

The Learning Process

Before we go on to learn about the teaching skills that facilitate learning, we should understand the learning process (Ausebel, Novak and Havesian, 1978; Bloom, 1971; Dewey, 1910; Dollard and Miller, 1950; Gagne, 1977; Guilford, 1967; Pavlov, 1957; Piaget, 1950, 1952; Piaget and Inhelder, 1969). In order for us to say that learning has occurred, there must be some kind of a demonstration of gain or change in behavior. The process out of which this learned behavior occurs may be mediated by human intelligence. When it is not mediated by human intelligence, we say that the behavior was "conditioned." That is, the stimulus and response were associated and reinforced in such a way that either may evoke the other upon its appearance, without being processed by human intelligence.

When the behavior is mediated by intelligence, we may say that true learning has occurred. That is, the learners were involved in a learning process that enabled them to use their intelligence in describing the causes, predicting the effects and demonstrating the behavioral gain or change needed to achieve and use the effects. At the highest levels of intelligence, the learners are not only involved in such a learning process through the guidance of teachers, but also become equipped with the learning-to-learn skills they need to involve and move through the process independently.

Human Learning—Instrumental and Conditioned

A great deal depends upon how we develop our human resources. For example, it depends upon how the environment—which is largely human—interacts with our biological selves. We can see this most clearly in the first year of a child's life. The newborn infant enters the world with few skills other than physiological reflex responses. Thus, for example, the child has the sucking reflex and the palmar or grasping reflex.

If the environment is responsive to the child, these reflexes will become instrumental to the child's survival. They constitute the child's initial movements toward the world which will lead, ultimately, to his or her growth and development. The child will be able to nurse with the sucking reflex. Later on, the child will be able to manipulate things with the grasping reflex.

In the beginning, however, newborn infants bring little but their inherent resources to their worlds. In their utter dependency, they wait for us to insure their survival by responding to their needs, and by gradually guiding them to the things they need to have to maintain themselves.

Habits—Conditioned Responses

One of the ways that we guide our children is by helping them to form habits (Dollard and Miller, 1950; Pavlov, 1957). Basically, human habits are behaviors that are acquired without human intelligence. They can be acquired by associating or relating, in space and time, two or more sets of activities. At least one of these activities must satisfy some human need in order for the behavior to be repeated as a habit. For example, the child may develop the sucking habit when nourished by the mother's breast. The results may be said to be instrumental in satisfying the child's need for nourishment.

In the process, the child may develop a "conditioned" sucking response to the stimulus of the mother's nipple. In a similar manner, the child later on may develop a conditioned grasping response to the stimulus of food, which is instrumental in satisfying the child's need for nourishment. There are many other kinds of life habits which can be developed without human intelligence or intentionality.

The learning theorists write of these habits in terms of classical, instrumental, and other kinds of conditioning. The habits are "learned" only in the sense that they are repeated. They are not learned in the sense of being the product of human understanding. In fact, these habits are conditioned spinal responses, not learned responses. Indeed, most of what we teach about learning is based upon what we know about conditioning. This is precisely why we know so little about learning.

Exploration—The First Phase of Learning
Human learning and, indeed, human intelligence begin to manifest themselves when children are several months old. At this point, children begin to explore themselves and their environments. They discover the existence of and the relationships between environmental stimuli and their own responses. In other terms, the children become aware of the association of the stimuli to which they have become conditioned and the responses which have been conditioned to the stimuli. They become aware of causes and effects in their worlds.

This awareness is a two-way street. For example, the child becomes aware that the nipple or the food serves as stimulus to a sucking or grasping response. This response, in turn, will lead to satisfying a need for nourishment. The child may also become aware that a need for nourishment stimulates the response of search for the nipple or the food.

In summary, through exploring, children become aware of both their past and present relationships to their environments—including themselves. Children attempt to describe where they are in relation to themselves and the worlds around them. **Exploring** is the first stage or phase of human learning. This form of exploration begins to distinguish humankind from all other forms of life.

Understanding—The Second Phase of Learning

It is a short step from becoming aware of the ingredients of human experience to anticipating experiences. With an increasing confidence in this awareness of the relationship of stimulus and response, the child is prepared for instrumental or purposeful learning at about one year of age. In other words, the child sets out to obtain a certain result or end, independent of the means to be employed. For example, the child may set out to attract its mother, or to obtain food or an object that is out of reach.

Drawing from this awareness of the relationship between stimulus and response or cause and effect, the child sets a goal of achieving certain effects. The goals of the instrumental act are often only seen later although some approximation of them was obviously intended from the beginning.

In summary, children understand their relationships to future events or experiences. They are, in effect, attempting to predict the consequences of their efforts. They understand where they want to be in their worlds. This **understanding** is the second stage or phase of human learning. It is what allows humankind to anticipate its future—another distinction from other forms of life.

Action—The Third Phase of Learning

The next phase of human learning flows naturally from the understanding phase. It involves the development of behavioral patterns instrumental to achieving goals. From the end of the first year onwards, the child draws from his or her repertoire of behaviors to produce the responses needed to achieve a goal. For example, the child may laugh or cry to bring the mother or surrogate to him or her. The child may move his or her hand in the direction of the unreachable food or object. There may be a series of trial and error experiences. These experiences may either confirm the child's responses, through reaching the goal and experiencing satisfaction, or else they may reject the child's responses, through not reaching the goal.

In summary, children begin to act in order to get from where they are to where they want to be within their worlds. They are, in effect, attempting to control themselves and their worlds. **Acting** is the third stage or phase of learning. It enables human beings to plan and work towards the end of influencing their future.

Human Growth—A Learning Prototype

The first year of human development serves as a prototype for all human learning (Carkhuff and Berenson, 1981). The child's reflexes are unknowingly conditioned as habitual responses to certain stimuli. These habits serve as the limited repertoire of responses with which the child initially approaches the world. Improvement in the quantity and quality of responses with which the learner ultimately relates to the world depends upon the development of the child's intelligence. This, in turn, depends upon how effectively he or she goes through the stages or phases of learning.

Initially, the child explores and identifies the nature of the stimuli and responses in his or her experience. Transitionally, the child comes to understand the interactive nature of stimuli and responses, anticipates the effects of one upon the other and develops goals to achieve these effects. Finally, the child acts by drawing from his or her developing repertoire of responses to attempt to achieve goals. The child's action behavior is shaped by feedback or by the effects it achieves. This feedback recycles the stages or phases of learning as the child explores more extensively, understands more accurately and acts more effectively. This ascending, enlarging spiral of exploration, understanding and action is the source of the adult's improving repertoire of responses.

What goes on in the first year of life continues in more and more refined ways throughout life—or not. How effectively we live our lives depends totally upon how efficiently and effectively we learn (Carkhuff and Berenson, 1981).

The Skills of Exploring—An Intuitive Activity
Just watch the learners' exploratory activities. Perhaps we can see these in a classroom most clearly in the absence of formal teaching. The learners may become interested in some object or mechanism on their own initiative in the absence of a teacher. The learners will approach the material or object and position themselves so as to give it their attention. They may observe the thing for a while, perhaps listen to it and then probably touch it. The touching will lead to handling. The learners may try it out in different ways, turning the material around or over, or attaching it to other things.

The learners may try to figure out what the thing is and does, and maybe even why and how it does it. Finally, they may try to do whatever it does. In the process, they have found out what they know about it, and what they can do with it. In short, they have found out where they are in relation to the learning experience. (So have their teachers, if they are present.)

The learners must address all sources of learning in a similar manner. If the teacher is presenting some content in the classroom, the learners must use all of their exploring skills to address the teacher, the content, the delivery or method, and the classroom environment as dimensions of the learning experience. Learners must also address themselves as potential sources of learning, in terms of the learning experiences and learning skills that they bring to the learning process. By exploring all dimensions of the learning experience, the learners can find out where they are in relation to the learning experience. They will then be ready to find out where they want to be.

The Skills of Understanding—A Mediating Activity
The learners may engage in a series of understanding activities. They may relate the dimensions of their current experiences to those of their past experiences. They may organize the dimensions of these experiences in different ways based upon their similarities and differences. The learners may organize the dimensions of the learning experience in still different ways based upon their functions and the values of these functions to their learning. The learners may generalize their needs for these values, and set generalized learning goals based upon the learning experience and specific learning objectives derived from the different dimensions of the learning experience. Or they may do

all of this, by simply determining what, of all the content possible, they have yet to learn.

Where there is a teacher with a teaching goal, all of these activities can take place in relation to the teaching goal. The learners may set their learning objectives in relation to the teaching goals. Where there is no teacher, the learners may set their learning objectives based upon their generalized needs. In summary, the learners gain increasing confidence in their understanding of where they are in relation to where they want to be. They are ready to act in order to get there.

The Skills of Acting—A Culminating Activity
Observing the learner in the action phase reveals the types of activities in which learners engage. First, they work to master the knowledge and skills involved in the learning goals. If the teachers have established the goal, they learn the knowledge or skills the teachers have developed. If teachers are not involved, learners can begin to define their skills objectives in terms of the deficits or problems they are having in achieving their goals, and to develop and implement programs designed to achieve those objectives.

In either event, having acquired the learning, the learners can repeat or practice the skill involved until it is ready and effectively available to them. Then they can apply it, either in some way that was intended by the teacher, or that is relevant to their own experience. They can continue to apply it in real-life, everyday living, learning, playing and working experiences. Finally, they can transfer the learning to unique and creative situations in their lives. This is the culmination of mastery: to be able to create with what you have learned.

Human Learning—A Growth Process

The learning voyage, then, begins where the learners are. Before our learners can embark upon their learning journeys, they must be able to identify the degrees of longitude and latitude at their points of origin. In terms of the learning process, they must know precisely where they are in relation to the learning experience. In order to do this, they must explore where they are. Learner **exploration** is the first phase of learning.

PHASE I OF LEARNING

EXPLORING
Where They Are

When the learners know where they are, then they can determine their ports of destination. They must know the degrees of longitude and latitude of their objectives. In terms of the learning process, the learners must understand where they are in relation to where they want to be, and also what they will need to obtain from the learning experience in order to get there. Learner **understanding** is the second phase of learning.

PHASES OF LEARNING

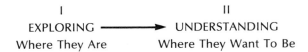

I	II
EXPLORING ⟶	UNDERSTANDING
Where They Are	Where They Want To Be

Finally, when the learners have established their ports of destination clearly in mind, they can begin their learning voyages. When they understand where they are in relation to where they want to be, they can act in order to get there. In other words, they can develop their own individualized learning processes, designed to achieve their learning objectives. Learner **acting** is the third phase of learning.

PHASES OF LEARNING

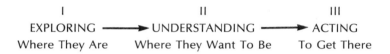

I	II	III
EXPLORING ———▶	UNDERSTANDING ———▶	ACTING
Where They Are	Where They Want To Be	To Get There

All productive learning is recycled. The learners receive feedback from acting. The feedback stimulates more extensive exploration; more accurate understanding; more effective action. The recycling intensifies the learning experience. For healthy and growing people it continues throughout life in an upwardly expanding spiral of learning.

PHASES OF LEARNING

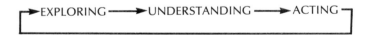

EXPLORING ———▶ UNDERSTANDING ———▶ ACTING

Teaching—The Basis of Learning
Learning is like a voyage. The learners will be transported from one port to another. The learning experience is the ship that will carry the learners. The teacher is the captain of the ship. All of the captain's skills must, therefore, relate directly to the passenger's welfare.

Everything the teacher does must directly facilitate the learners' movements through the learning process. At all stages of learning the teacher must be guided by what is effective for the learner. In the end, the teachers' effectiveness will be determined by their ability to facilitate the learners' recycling of learning in a life-long learning process. How the teaching skills relate directly to learners' movements through the learning process is the exciting topic of "An Introduction to Instruction," Volume II of *The Productive Teacher*.

Overview

In Volume I, "An Introduction to Curriculum Development," we concentrated upon preparing the content for the teaching delivery. In terms of the teaching triad (see Figure 1-1), the emphasis upon content is the first leg of the triad.

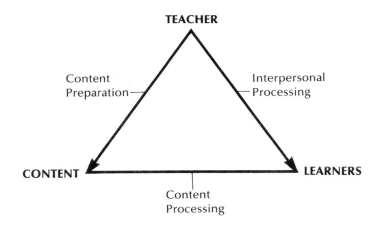

Figure **1-1.** The Teaching Triad

In the second leg, the teaching task is to relate the content to the learners and, in turn, the learners to the content. We may call the skills involved in relating the content to the learners teaching delivery skills.

In the third leg of the teaching triad, the teaching task is to relate to the learner in order to relate the learners to the content and, in turn, the teacher. We may call the skills involved in relating to the learners' frames of reference interpersonal processing skills.

When the teachers employ the content and interpersonal processing skills simultaneously while implementing their teaching delivery plan, we may conceive of the teachers as managing the learners' learning.

Together, the content and interpersonal processing skills in conjunction with the teaching delivery plan constitute the teaching delivery skills (TDS) of Volume II.

We can get a preview of the teaching delivery skills (TDS) of Volume II by looking at the teaching delivery process (See Figure 1-2). As can be seen, the

PHASES OF LEARNING

PRE-LEARNING	I	II	III

TEACHER:

CPS   Learning Management Plan

IPS

LEARNERS: ⟶ EXPLORE ⟶ UNDERSTAND ⟶ ACT

Figure 1-2. The Teaching Process Skills Facilitating Learning

TDS serve to facilitate the learners' movements through exploring, understanding and acting. Before we begin teaching, we translate our teaching delivery plan into a learning management plan (Chapter 2). We then employ our content processing skills (CPS) to relate the content to the learners (Chapter 3). Similarly, we use our interpersonal processing skills (IPS) to relate the learners to the content (Chapter 4). When employed simultaneously in implementing our learning management plan, our CPS and IPS are incorporated in our learning management skills (LMS) (Chapter 5). Finally, we evaluate our teaching (Chapter 6).

As can be seen, the learning management plan is prepared prior to using our teaching delivery skills (TDS) in order to make the teaching delivery. All of this content development and organization effort occurs prior to involving the learners in learning. Content preparation is a necessary but not sufficient condition of making a teaching delivery. It remains for us to learn the productive teaching delivery skills that will make us productive teachers in the Age of Information. Making a productive teaching delivery is the topic of Volume II, "An Introduction to Instruction."

24

References

Aspy, D. N., Aspy, C. B. and Roebuck, F. N. *The Third Century in American Education.* Amherst, MA: Human Resource Development Press, 1984.

Ausebel, D., Novak, J., and Havesian, H. *Educational Psychology.* New York: Holt, Rinehart and Winston, 1978.

Bloom, B. S. *Mastery Learning: Theory and Practice.* New York: Holt, Rinehart and Winston, 1971.

Carkhuff, R. R. *Human Processing.* Amherst, MA: Carkhuff Institute of Human Technology, 1984(b).

Carkhuff, R. R. *Productivity Processing.* Amherst, MA: Carkhuff Institute of Human Technology, in press, 1984(b).

Carkhuff, R. R. and Berenson, D. H. *The Skilled Teacher.* Amherst, MA: Human Resource Development Press, 1981.

Dewey, J. *How We Think.* Boston: D.C. Heath, 1910.

Dollard, J. and Miller, N. *Personality and Psychotherapy.* New York: McGraw-Hill, 1950.

Gagne, R. M. *Condition of Learning.* New York: Holt, Rinehart and Winston, 1977.

Guilford, J. P. *The Nature of Human Intelligence.* New York: Holt, Rinehart and Winston, 1967.

Pavlov, I. *Experimental Psychology.* New York: Philosophical History, 1957.

Piaget, J. *The Psychology of Intelligence.* London: Routledge and Kegan Paul, 1950.

Piaget, J. *The Origins of Intelligence in Children.* New York: International Universities Press, 1952.

Piaget, J. and Inhelder, B. *The Psychology of the Child.* New York: Basic Books, 1969.

2.
Planning for Learning Management

Contrary to popular opinion, the teacher's primary task is not that of "mother of the classroom." Nor is it cleaning up, arranging or decorating the class-room, parading through a textbook, or even presenting the learning material itself. Indeed, the teacher's primary task is not "teaching." *The teacher's primary task is managing learning.* Like the captain of the learn-ing ship, the teacher must know the degrees of latitude and longitude for which the boat is headed. The teacher must also be the chief operations officer on this learning ship, i.e., to be able to perform all of the operations necessary to bring the ship to all the rele-vant living, learning and working ports of life. But the learners are not mere passengers anymore. In the Age of Information, they are now learning apprentices. In-deed, along the way they will learn to share teaching as well as learning responsibilities. They now need to learn a set of learning skills and the contents which that yields. They will need to share in the instructional systems design and teaching delivery of their own con-tent. At their most mature, the learners will need to be able to do everything that the teacher does. Along the way, as they move from and to the ports of content, the learning of these apprentices must be managed by the teacher. To be sure, it is most helpful to conceive of the teacher as a learning manager rather than as a teacher in a traditional sense.

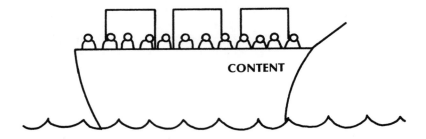

The Learning Voyage

When teachers plan for managing learning, they emphasize the conditions that maximize learning (Berenson, Berenson and Carkhuff, 1978; Carkhuff and Berenson, 1981). The content is developed to emphasize the skill steps that achieve the skill objective (French, et al, 1957; Kearney, 1953; Lumsdaine, 1964; Mager, 1962; Smith and Moore, 1962). The content is organized to emphasize exercising the skill steps leading to the skill application (A.E.R.A., 1966; McCullough, 1963; SCRDT, 1976). The teaching methods are developed to emphasize the kinesthetic skill steps; i.e., those steps that the learners actually do or perform (Berliner, 1977; Gage, 1976, 1977). Together, the content development, content organization and teaching methods converge to emphasize learner skill applications based upon learner skill acquisitions which, in turn, are based upon learner skill step exercises. It is the teacher's primary task to manage the learning process. To do this, the teacher must develop the learning management plan.

Principles of Learning Management Planning

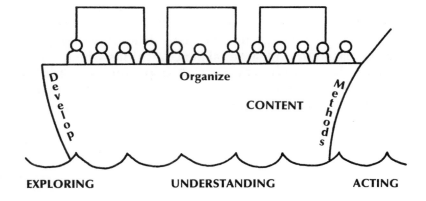

EXPLORING   UNDERSTANDING   ACTING

The Learning Process

Our teaching objective in this lesson is as follows:

The teachers will develop learning management planning skills by designing the learning management plan under formal and informal conditions at levels that enable the learners to perform skill applications.

Before you learn to develop learning management planning skills, you may want an index of your skills in this area. Perhaps you can develop a teaching delivery plan for achieving your skill objective in your specialty skill content. Outline how you would develop and organize your content and integrate the content and teaching methods.

_____

_____

_____

_____

_____

Indexing Learning Management Planning Skills

You did well if you emphasized the teaching delivery plan. The delivery plan includes the levels of skills content, the sequence of content organization and the modalities of teaching methods. Thus, the delivery plan emphasizes reviewing the contingency skills (CS); overviewing the skill applications (SA); presenting and exercising the skill steps (SS); and summarizing the skill performance (SP).

CONTENT DEVELOPMENT:	Skills, Skill Steps, Supportive Knowledge
CONTENT ORGANIZATION:	Review, Overview, Present, Exercise, Summarize
TEACHING METHODS:	**Tell, Show, Do (Repeat, Apply)**

CONTENT ORGANIZATION

TEACHING METHODS	REVIEW	OVERVIEW	PRESENT	EXERCISE	SUMMARIZE
TELL	CS	SA	SS	SS	SP
SHOW	CS	SA	SS	SS	SP
DO	CS	SA	SS	SS	SP

Overviewing Learning Management Planning Skills

Planning Review Management
In planning to manage learning during the review, the teacher emphasizes the learners' performance. Remember, the review yields a pre-instructional index of the learners' levels of functioning. Thus, the teacher emphasizes the learners' performance of contingency skills: do the learners have the skills upon which the new skills are based? The teacher manages learning during the review by providing the opportunity for the learners to **tell, show** and **do** the skills: as the learners are performing the contingency skills, they are describing and modeling the skill steps and knowledge involved.

CONTENT PHASE:	Review
CONTENT LEVEL:	Contingency Skill Performance
TEACHING METHODS:	Learner **Tell-Show-Do**

Planning Review Learning

For example, in our learning skills curriculum, we have a skill objective of exploring the learning experience. Exploring is comprised of analyzing and responding skills. Before proceeding, we need to get an index of the learners' involving skills. The learners may **tell-show-do** the skills comprising the learning involving skills.

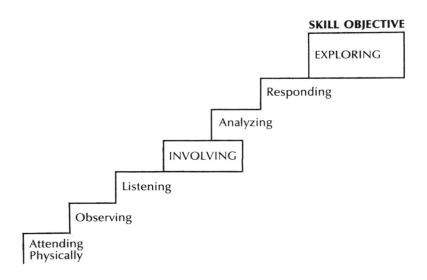

SKILL OBJECTIVE

EXPLORING

Responding

Analyzing

INVOLVING

Listening

Observing

Attending
Physically

LEARNING OBJECTIVE: Exploring
CONTINGENCY SKILL: Involving
LEARNER TELL-SHOW-DO: Attending, observing, listening

Reviewing Learner Contingency Skills

The following example for the skill objective of producing a flow chart shows the learner **tell-show-do** steps required for the review.

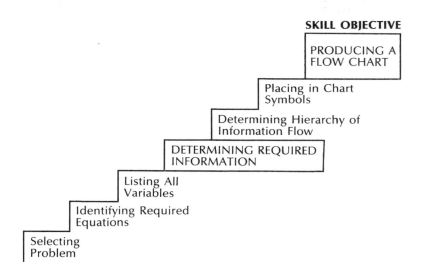

SKILL OBJECTIVE

PRODUCING A FLOW CHART

Placing in Chart Symbols

Determining Hierarchy of Information Flow

DETERMINING REQUIRED INFORMATION

Listing All Variables

Identifying Required Equations

Selecting Problem

LEARNING OBJECTIVES: Producing a flow chart
CONTINGENCY SKILL: Determining required information
LEARNER TELL-SHOW-DO: Selecting problem, identifying required equations, listing all variables

Repeating Again...

34

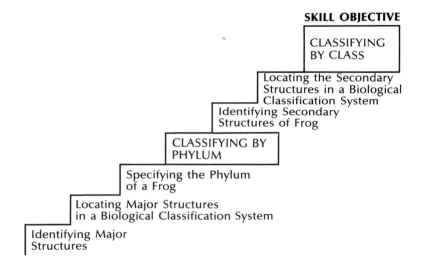

CLASSIFYING
BY CLASS

Locating the Secondary
Structures in a Biological
Classification System

Identifying Secondary
Structures of Frog

CLASSIFYING BY
PHYLUM

Specifying the Phylum
of a Frog

Locating Major Structures
in a Biological Classification System

Identifying Major
Structures

...And Again

You may practice planning review management in your specialty content. Simply outline your review objective, contingency skill and the learner **tell-show-do** to be performed.

LEARNING OBJECTIVE:

_____

_____

_____

CONTINGENCY SKILL:

_____

_____

_____

LEARNER TELL-SHOW-DO:

_____

_____

_____

Exercising Review Planning

Planning Overview Management

The teacher is a participant in managing learning during the overview. The overview is an opportunity to compare images of the potential skill applications of the skill to be learned. The overview gives the teacher an opportunity to demonstrate expertise. It provides the learners with an opportunity to become motivated to learn the skill. Accordingly, both teacher and learners offer their images of prospective skill applications. They both do so by **telling-showing-doing** the skill applications. Hopefully, both teacher and learners will have their repertoires of skill applications expanded. Hopefully, both teacher and learners will be motivated to become involved in the learning process.

CONTENT PHASE:	Overview
CONTENT LEVEL:	Skill applications
TEACHING METHODS:	Teacher and learner **tell-show-do**

Planning Overview Learning

For example, in our learning skills curriculum, our overview objective is exploring. The potential skill applications may be drawn from living, learning and working arenas. Both teachers and learners may demonstrate their expertise by illustrating exploring components and/or functions and/or processes in the different arenas.

OVERVIEW OBJECTIVE: Exploring

SKILL APPLICATIONS: Living, learning, working applications

TEACHER & LEARNER
TELL-SHOW-DO: Analyzing and responding

Overviewing Learner Skill Applications

For another example, a computer programming curriculum overview objective might be constructing a flow chart. The skill applications can utilize problems from living, learning and working areas. Teachers and learners may illustrate their skills by flow charting problems based on components and/or functions and/or processes.

OVERVIEW OBJECTIVE:	Constructing a flow chart
SKILL APPLICATIONS:	Living, learning, working applications
TEACHER & LEARNER **TELL-SHOW-DO:**	Selecting problems, identifying required equations, listing all variables

Repeating Again...

In the science curriculum, an overview objective is classifying. Skill applications can be drawn from living, learning and working areas.

OVERVIEW OBJECTIVE: Classifying

SKILL APPLICATION: Systematic categorization in living, learning and working applications

TEACHER & LEARNER TELL-SHOW-DO: Identifying and comparing

. . . And Again

You may practice planning overview management in your specialty content. Simply outline your overview objective, skill applications, and the teacher's and learner's **tell-show-do.**

OVERVIEW OBJECTIVE:

_____

_____

_____

SKILL APPLICATION:

_____

_____

_____

TEACHER & LEARNER TELL-SHOW-DO:

_____

_____

_____

Exercising Overview Planning

Planning Presentation Management

The teacher takes his or her most active role in presenting. Still, the purpose of the presentation is for the learner to perform the skill steps. Even during the teacher's **telling** and **showing** the skill steps, the emphasis is upon the learners' **doing** the skill steps. Thus, both teacher and learners share differentially in the presentation. The teacher **tells** and **shows** the skill steps so that the learners can **do** the skill steps. Hopefully, the teacher will have didactically taught and modeled the skill steps effectively enough to facilitate the learners experientially doing the steps. The teacher can further "shape" the learners' performances by differentially reinforcing the skill steps performed.

CONTENT PHASE:	Present
CONTENT LEVEL:	Skill steps
TEACHING METHODS:	Teacher **tell-show**, learner **do**

Planning Presentation Learning

For example, in our learning skills curriculum, our presentation objective is analyzing the learning experience. The skill steps involve analyzing the components, functions and processes of the learning experience. The teacher **tells** and **shows** analyzing what the exercise is (components), what it does (functions) and how it does it (processes). The learner performs the **do** step: analyzing the learning experience.

> **PRESENTATION OBJECTIVE:** Analyzing learning experience
>
> **SKILL STEPS:** Analyzing components, functions, and processes
>
> **TEACHER TELL & SHOW:** Analyzing what it is and does and how it does it
>
> **LEARNER DO:** Analyzing what it is and does and how it does it

Presenting Learner Skill Steps

A computer programming skills curriculum might include a presentation objective of writing assignment statements. The skill steps would involve identifying the components, functions, and processes of assignment statements. The teacher **tells** and **shows** what assignment statements are, what they do and how they do it. The learner performs the **do** step: writing assignment statements.

PRESENTATION OBJECTIVE:	Writing assignment statements
SKILL STEPS:	Identifying components, functions and processes
TEACHER TELL & SHOW:	Identifying what they are and do and how they do it
LEARNER DO:	Writing assignment statements

Repeating Again...

Similarly, in the science skills curriculum a presentation objective might be identifying major homologous structures. The skill steps include identifying components, functions and processes of major homologous structures.

PRESENTATION OBJECTIVE:	Identifying major homologous structures
SKILL STEPS:	Identifying components, functions and processes
TEACHER TELL & SHOW:	Identifying what it is and does and how it does it
LEARNER DO:	Identifying what it is and where it belongs

...And Again

You may practice planning presentation management in your specialty content. Simply outline your presentation objective, skill steps and the teacher's and learners' **tell-show-do's.**

PRESENTATION OBJECTIVE:

_____

_____

_____

SKILL STEPS:

_____

_____

_____

TEACHER & LEARNER TELL-SHOW-DO:

_____

_____

_____

Exercising Presentation Planning

Planning Exercise Management

The exclusive emphasis in the exercise is again upon the learners. The teacher manages the learners' exercising the skill steps. Again, the learners' **tell-show-do** the skill steps until they have demonstrated expertise in their performance. This means that the learners **repeat** the skill steps until they have acquired them. Moreover, it means that they **apply** the skill steps by practicing increasing approximations of real-life applications until they are able to make them effectively and efficiently.

CONTENT PHASE:	Exercise
CONTENT LEVEL:	Skill steps
TEACHING METHODS:	Learner **tell-show-do**

Planning Exercise Learning

For example, in our learning skills curriculum, our exercising objective is again analyzing the learning experience. The skill steps also involve analyzing the components, functions and processes of the learning experience. The learners **tell-show-do** analyzing the components, functions, and processes of a learning experience.

EXERCISING OBJECTIVE:	Analyzing learning experience
SKILL STEPS:	Analyzing components, functions, and processes
LEARNER TELL-SHOW-DO:	Analyzing what it is and does and how it does it

Exercising Learner Skill Steps

Exercising provides an opportunity to practice the new skills. An exercising objective for the computer programming curriculum involves writing assignment statements, which was our previous presentation objective. The learners **tell-show-do** identifying the functions, components, and processes of writing assignment statements.

EXERCISING OBJECTIVE:	Writing assignment statements
SKILL STEPS:	Identifying components, functions and processes
LEARNER TELL-SHOW-DO:	Identifying what they are and how they do it

Repeating Again...

Utilizing the science curriculum example, our exercising objective might consist of identifying and categorizing homologous structures. The learner would **tell, show** and **do** the identifying of the homologous structures.

EXERCISING OBJECTIVE:	Identifying and categorizing homologous structures
SKILL STEPS:	Identifying components, functions and processes
LEARNER TELL-SHOW-DO:	Identifying what it is and does and where it belongs

...And Again

You may practice planning exercise management in your specialty content. Simply outline your exercising objective, skill steps and the learners' **tell-show-do.**

EXERCISING OBJECTIVE:

_____

_____

_____

SKILL STEPS:

_____

_____

_____

LEARNER TELL-SHOW-DO:

_____

_____

_____

Exercising Exercise Planning

Planning Summary Management
The summary emphasizes learning management just as the review did. The summary yields a post-instructional index of the learners' levels of functioning. Thus, the teacher emphasizes the learners' performance of the skills. Again, the teacher manages learning during the review by providing the opportunity for the learners to **tell-show-do** the skills. Hopefully, this post-teaching index will relate to the learners' real-life living, learning, and working applications.

CONTENT PHASE: Summary
CONTENT LEVEL: Skill performance
TEACHING METHODS: Learner **tell-show-do**

Planning Summary Learning

For example, in our learning skills curriculum, our summarizing objective is analyzing. The skill to be performed is analyzing the learning experience. The learners **tell-show-do** analyzing the components, functions, and processes of a learning experience.

SUMMARIZING OBJECTIVE: Analyzing
SKILL PERFORMANCE: Analyzing learning experience
LEARNER TELL-SHOW-DO: Analyzing components, functions, and processes

Summarizing Learner Skill Performance

The summarizing objective for the computer programming example is writing. The summarizing skill is writing assignment statements. This demonstration of the skill provides not only an index of skill acquisition, but also the opportunity to relate the skill to real life applications.

SUMMARIZING OBJECTIVE: Writing
SKILL PERFORMANCE: Writing assignment statements
LEARNER TELL-SHOW-DO: Identifying/writing components, functions, and processes

Repeating Again...

In this example, the summarizing objective is identifying and the skill to be performed is that of identifying major homologous structures. The learner must **tell, show** and **do** identifying components; functions and processes.

SUMMARIZING OBJECTIVE: Identifying
SKILL PERFORMANCE: Identifying major homologous structures
LEARNER TELL-SHOW-DO: Identifying components, functions, and processes

...And Again

You may practice planning summary management learning in your specialty content. Simply outline your summarizing objective, skill to be performed, and the learners' **tell-show-do**.

SUMMARIZING OBJECTIVE:

_____

_____

_____

SKILL PERFORMANCE:

_____

_____

_____

LEARNER TELL-SHOW-DO:

_____

_____

_____

Exercising Summary Planning

Exercising

You now know how to plan learning management in making your teaching delivery. Later we will use our learning management skills to teach any new material while "thinking on our feet," in or out of the classroom. We can apply our learning management planning skills in any critical situation that involves teaching and learning. For example, we could employ learning management planning skills for teaching parents to observe their children at home. Or we can teach our learners to manage their own learning.

SKILL OBJECTIVE:	Learners will manage their learning by using learning management skills under classroom conditions at 90% level of effective applications.
CONTENT PHASES:	Review, overview, present, exercise, summarize
CONTENT LEVELS:	Skills, skill steps and supportive knowledge
TEACHING METHODS:	**Tell-show-do (repeat-apply)**

Exercising Learning Management Planning Skills

You may wish to repeat planning learning management exercises. Apply the exploring skills objective to living or working skills contexts at home or on-the-job. Develop your content phases, levels, teaching methods and learner management and teacher responsibilities.

SKILL OBJECTIVE: _____

_____

_____

CONTENT PHASES: _____

_____

CONTENT LEVELS: _____

_____

TEACHING METHODS: _____

_____

LEARNER MANAGEMENT: _____

_____

Repeating Learning Management Planning

Try to make a variety of living, learning and working learning management applications with your specialty skills content:

_____

_____

_____

_____

_____

_____

_____

_____

_____

_____

Applying Learning Management Planning

Summarizing

Perhaps you can again develop your teaching delivery plan for achieving your skill objective in your specialty skill content. Outline how you would develop and organize your content and integrate the content and teaching methods.

_____

_____

_____

_____

_____

You will feel confident if you are able to develop your teaching delivery plan effectively. Then we will have achieved our skill objective:

> The teachers will develop learning management planning skills by designing the learning management plan under formal and informal conditions at levels that enable the learners to perform skill applications.

Indexing Learning Management Planning Skills

You will feel very good about your learning man-agement planning skills if you emphasized managing the learners' learning. Again, your delivery plan in-cludes the levels of skills content, the sequence of con-tent organization, and the modalities of teaching methods.

CONTENT DEVELOPMENT:	Skills, skill steps, and supportive knowledge
CONTENT ORGANIZATION:	Review, overview, present, exercise, summarize
TEACHING METHODS:	**Tell, show, do (repeat, apply)**

While emphasizing specific levels of skills, all dimen-sions of content and methods potentially interact with all other dimensions.

CONTENT ORGANIZATION

TEACHING METHODS	REVIEW	OVERVIEW	PRESENT	EXERCISE	SUMMARIZE
TELL	L	T & L	T	L	L
SHOW	L	T & L	T	L	L
DO	L	T & L	L	L	L

Summarizing Learning Management Planning

Yes, the teacher is the captain and chief operations officer on the learning ship. As the teacher manages the learners' learning, the learners will assume increasing responsibilities for the performance of the ship as well as themselves. With the constantly changing data inputs of the Information Age, the learners must participate in their own instructional design. They must learn to develop their own teaching delivery plans. Transitionally, they must learn to make their own teaching deliveries to themselves as well as others. This will prepare them for life after formal educational experiences. Gradually, the teacher must release the authority that goes with the responsibilities the learners can assume. Ultimately, the teacher must relinquish the control that enables the learners to help to guide the learning ship from port of content to port of content. Hopefully, we will lose no passengers along the way but will facilitate the development of a host of crew members and future captains.

References

American Educational Research Association. *Review of Educational Research.* Washington, DC: AERA, 1966.

Berenson, S. R., Berenson, D. H. and Carkhuff, R. R. *The Skills of Teaching—Lesson Planning Skills.* Amherst, MA: Human Resource Development Press, 1978.

Berliner, D. C. *Instructional Time in Research on Teaching.* San Fransisco, CA: Far West Laboratory for Educational Research and Development, 1977.

Carkhuff, R. R. and Berenson, D. H. *The Skilled Teacher.* Amherst, MA: Human Resource Development Press, 1981.

French, W. and Associates. *Behavioral Goals of General Education in High School.* New York, NY: Russell Sage Foundation, 1957.

Gage, N. L., Editor. *The Psychology of Teaching Methods.* Chicago, IL: University of Chicago Press, 1976.

Gage, N. L. *The Scientific Basis of the Art of Teaching.* New York, NY: Teachers College Press, 1977.

Kearney, N. C. *Elementary School Objectives.* New York, NY: Russell Sage Foundation, 1953.

Lumsdaine, A. A. "Educational Technology, Programmed Learning and Instructional Science." In *Theories of Learning and Instruction,* National Society for the Study of Education, 63rd Yearbook, Part 1, Chicago, IL: University of Chicago Press, 1964.

Mager, R. F. *Preparing Instructional Objectives.* San Fransisco, CA: Fearon Publishers, 1962.

McCullough, C. M. "What Does Research Reveal About Practices in Teaching Reading?" In *Handbook of Research on Teaching.* N. L. Gage, Editor. Chicago, IL: Rand McNally, 1963.

SCRDT, *Program on Teaching Effectiveness.* Stanford, CA: Stanford Center for Research and Development in Teaching, 1976.

Smith, W. I. and Moore, J. W. "Size of Step and Caring." *Psychological Reports,* 1962, *10,* 287–294.

II.
TEACHING
DELIVERY
SKILLS

A pplying teaching skills is the core of the teaching-learning process. The teaching skills serve to facilitate the learners' movements through the exploring, understanding and acting phases of learning. The teaching skills chapters are organized around the basic principles of learning as follows:

Chapter 3—Content Processing Skills
All productive learning is broken down in atomistic steps of the skills content.

Chapter 4—Interpersonal Processing Skills
All productive learning begins with the learners' frames of reference.

Chapter 5—Learning Management Skills
All productive learning emphasizes content and interpersonal processing skills employed simultaneously with the learning management plan.

Applying teaching skills to facilitate the learning process is the essential task of making a teaching delivery.

3.
Content
Processing
Skills

The difference between those who teach content and those who teach learners is in their teaching delivery skills. For most of us, the teaching delivery is the most intense and rewarding moment in teaching: it brings the teacher into direct contact with the learners. We have prepared our content to deliver to our learners. We have prepared our delivery plans for making the teaching delivery. Now we funnel our content, organization and methods into the learning process in which we involve our learners. Again, the learning process involves the learners in *exploring* where they are with the content; *understanding* where they want or need to be; and *acting* to get to their learning goals. Teaching delivery skills facilitate the learners' movements through these phases of learning.

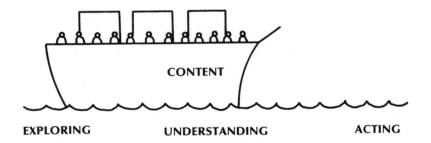

EXPLORING   UNDERSTANDING   ACTING

Content Delivery

The delivery of any content in any area of human endeavor requires both an external and an internal emphasis (Carkhuff and Berenson, 1981). The external emphasis represents the content to be delivered. It is based upon the recipients' movements through the levels of these skills (Berenson, Berenson, and Carkhuff, 1978a, 1978b). At each step of skills development the recipients' progress is assessed. Teachers are facilitative in delivering their content when they: 1) diagnose the learners in terms of their needs (Pfeiffer, 1966); 2) select and specify goals that are congruent with learners' needs (Flanders, 1960, 1963); 3) present the material in a highly cognitive and atomistic manner (Kaya, et al, 1967); and then 4) monitor the learning in terms of the goals that were specified (Clark, 1971; Hudgins, 1974). All of these functions are incorporated in teaching delivery skills.

Principles of Teaching Delivery

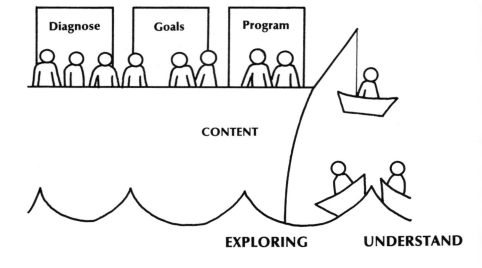

Content Processing Skills

Our CPS teaching objective in this lesson is as follows:

The teachers will make teaching deliveries by implementing content processing skills under formal and informal conditions at levels that facilitate the learners' process movements.

Before you learn CPS, you may want an index of your skills in this area. Perhaps you can take some teaching objective in your specialty content and outline the content processing by which you would facilitate its achievement.

_____

_____

_____

_____

_____

Indexing CPS

You will be pleased if you emphasized delivering the content to the learners. These CPS will include diagnosing the learners in terms of the content; setting goals based upon the diagnosis; programming based upon the goals; and monitoring based upon the programs.

PREPARING CONTENT: Preparing daily content in order to involve the learners in learning.

DIAGNOSING: Diagnosing learners' levels of functioning on content in order to facilitate learner exploration.

SETTING GOALS: Setting goals for skills and knowledge based upon diagnosis in order to facilitate learner understanding.

PROGRAMMING: Developing steps to achieve goals in order to facilitate learner acting.

MONITORING: Observing feedback from acting in order to facilitate learner recycling of the learning process.

PHASES OF LEARNING

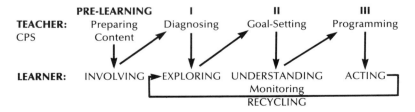

Overviewing CPS

Preparing Content

We have already attended to content preparation skills. We have developed our content, planned our deliveries and teaching methods and developed our learning management programs before coming into contact with the learners. In other words, preparing content takes place before learning ensues. The relationship between the prepared content and the phases of the teaching delivery is important to understand. The exploring-understanding-acting (E-U-A) learning process is an ongoing one. In making the teaching delivery, the E-U-A process is recycled for every stage of the delivery plan. Thus, the teacher is constantly diagnosing, setting goals, programming and monitoring in order to facilitate the learners' E-U-A process.

Preparing Content

Within every phase of learning management, the teacher facilitates the learners' E-U-A. For example, within the review of the learners' contingency skills, the teacher is using delivery skills to facilitate the learners' E-U-A: diagnosing the learners' functioning; setting goals based upon the diagnosis; developing programs based upon the goals; and monitoring the programs. Teaching delivery skills emphasize moment-to-moment programming for learning achievement. They make the learning process live. They make the delivery plan work.

CONTENT ORGANIZATION

TEACHING METHODS	REVIEW	OVERVIEW	PRESENT	EXERCISE	SUMMARIZE
TELL	L	T & L	T	L	L
SHOW	L	T & L	T	L	L
DO	L	T & L	L	L	L

L — Learners
T — Teacher

Managing Learning

You may wish to practice in imagery using content preparation skills to facilitate the learners' E-U-A within every phase of your learning management plan. Simply imagine yourself in different teaching situations demanding your content preparation skills. Be sure to emphasize using the teaching delivery skills within each phase of the plan.

Exercising Preparing Content

Diagnosing Learners

Diagnosing the learner is where the teaching delivery begins. The diagnosis lets us know where the learners are functioning in terms of the skills content. It also lets the learners know where they are beginning their learning experiences. By letting both teacher and learners know the point of the learners' entry into the learning experience, the diagnosis allows them to detail the teaching goals and programs. Most important, it allows both teacher and learners to tailor the learning of the content to the learners' unique needs. In other words, an accurate diagnosis is the basis for individualizing the learning process in terms of the learners' abilities to perform the skills content. In short, the diagnosis tells us the degrees of latitude and longitude from which the individual learners embark upon their learning journey. It enables us to determine precisely the degrees of latitude and longitude which we seek to achieve at our point of destination. Thus, the diagnostic process facilitates the learners' essential movements through the exploration phase of learning: exploring where they are in relation to the skills content. This provides the necessary conditions for movement to the next phase of learning: setting goals in order to facilitate the learners' understanding of where they are in relation to where they want or need to be.

Diagnosing

The essential question in diagnosis is: can the individual learners perform the skill? The implementation of the review enables us to make this functional diagnosis. If the learners can perform the skill, then they are ready to learn the next skill. For example, if the learners can analyze the learning experience then they are ready to learn the skills involved in responding to the learning experience. If the learners cannot analyze the learning experience, then we must assess the skill steps.

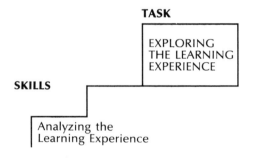

Assessing Skills

If, on the other hand, the learners cannot perform the skill, then we must discriminate the things they can do from those they cannot. After discrimination of skill performance, then, we must discriminate skill step performance. In other words, we must determine the number of steps which the learners can perform on the way to achievement of the skill. For example, if we are teaching analyzing as our learning skill, we may diagnose that an individual learner cannot perform the analyzing processes skill step. The level at which the learners perform the skill steps dictates the level at which we set the next skill objective.

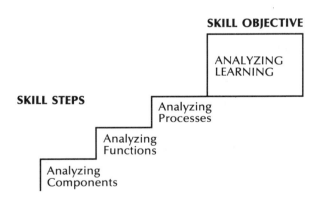

Assessing Skill Steps

If the learners cannot perform a given skill step, it may be because they lack the supportive knowledge. The next stage of diagnosing the learners, then, involves a diagnosis of their level of supportive knowledge. The learners may lack the facts and/or concepts and/or principles needed to perform the skill steps. For example, in analyzing processes the learner may lack the principle of analysis of learning that derives from analyzing processes: If the learners analyze processes, then they will be able to analyze the learning experience so that they can explore the learning experience fully.

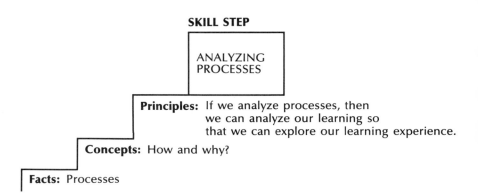

SKILL STEP

ANALYZING
PROCESSES

Principles: If we analyze processes, then
we can analyze our learning so
that we can explore our learning experience.

Concepts: How and why?

Facts: Processes

Assessing Supportive Knowledge

By establishing the supportive knowledge required for a skill step, the learner diagnosis will be more accurate. For example, constructing a flow chart is a skill step necessary for computer programming. If this skill cannot be mastered, it is possible that the facts or concepts or principles have not been acquired which are essential to the skill step.

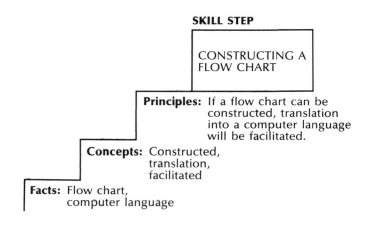

SKILL STEP

CONSTRUCTING A FLOW CHART

Principles: If a flow chart can be constructed, translation into a computer language will be facilitated.

Concepts: Constructed, translation, facilitated

Facts: Flow chart, computer language

Repeating Again...

Another example may help to clarify the process of assessing supportive knowledge. Before an animal can be classified in its biological phylum, its homologous structures must be identified. These are the essential facts. The essential concepts involve identification and classification. The principle states the relationship between the facts and concepts. Comprehension of each of these areas is essential before classification can be learned.

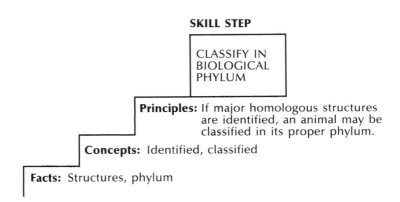

SKILL STEP

CLASSIFY IN
BIOLOGICAL
PHYLUM

Principles: If major homologous structures are identified, an animal may be classified in its proper phylum.

Concepts: Identified, classified

Facts: Structures, phylum

...And Again

The diagnosis should describe the learners' levels of functioning with regard to the skills and skill steps as well as the supportive knowledge. Both learners and teacher should have an observable index of the learners' performance. This enables both to know the point of entry into the learning experience. At this point, select a task, goal or skill objective for which you have developed your lesson plan and teaching methods. Develop your skill steps and supportive knowledge so that you can diagnose your learners' levels of functioning.

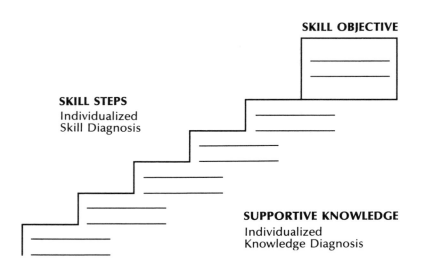

Exercising Diagnosing

Setting Learning Goals

The purpose of the diagnosis is to set goals for the learners. The diagnosis lets us know where the learners are functioning in terms of the skills content. Goal-setting lets us know where the learners are going to learn to function. Our goal-setting skills enable us to define and detail the learners' goals and objectives. The goals and objectives are within the grasp of the learners, because they are based upon accurate diagnoses of the learners. Most important, goal-setting enables both teacher and learners to focus upon goals that are tailored to the learners' unique needs. Again, the point of origin as well as the destination of the learning experience is known to the learners due to the teacher's diagnostic and goal-setting skills. The unique needs of the learners can be met in their special learning programs. Thus, our goal-setting process facilitates the learners' essential movements through the understanding phase of learning: understanding where they are in relation to where they want or need to be with the skills content. This provides the necessary conditions for movement to the next phase of learning: developing programs in order to facilitate the learners' action programs, to get them from where they are to where they want or need to be with the skills content.

Learning Goals

The essential question of goal-setting is similar to the diagnostic question: Can the learners potentially perform the skill? Obviously, the answer is based upon the skill diagnosis. Diagnosis of the learners' ability to perform the skill will determine the next level of skills goals. For example, if the learners can analyze the learning experience, then responding to the learning experience becomes the skill goal.

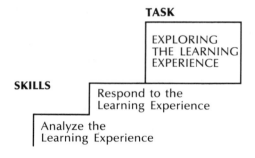

Setting Skill Objectives

After we have discriminated the skill performance of the learners, we must determine the next level of skill steps that the learners can learn to perform. For example, if we are teaching analyzing as our learning skill we may set an objective of analyzing processes for individual learners who we diagnose as being unable to perform that skill step. Again, the level at which the learners perform the skill steps dictates the level at which we set the next skill step objective.

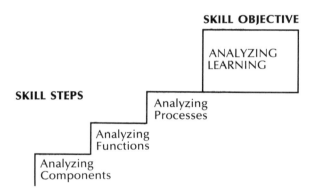

SKILL OBJECTIVE

ANALYZING
LEARNING

SKILL STEPS

Analyzing
Processes

Analyzing
Functions

Analyzing
Components

Setting Skill Step Objectives

If learners cannot perform a given skill step because they lack the supportive knowledge, then we must set goals for learning the supportive knowledge. For example, if the learners lack comprehension of the principle of analysis in learning, then the principle of analysis becomes the supportive knowledge goal: if the learners analyze the processes of the learning experience, then they will be able to analyze the learning experience so that they can explore the learning experience fully.

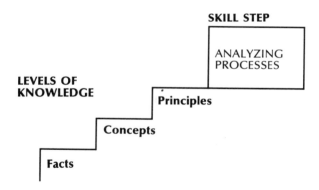

Setting Supportive Knowledge Goals

By diagnosing learner supportive knowledge, we are able to establish appropriate supportive knowledge goals. We may find that learners cannot construct a flow chart because they do not have the conceptual knowledge essential to the skill. Thus, this knowledge will become the supportive knowledge goal.

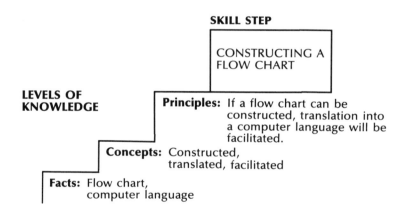

SKILL STEP

CONSTRUCTING A FLOW CHART

LEVELS OF KNOWLEDGE

Principles: If a flow chart can be constructed, translation into a computer language will be facilitated.

Concepts: Constructed, translated, facilitated

Facts: Flow chart, computer language

Repeating Again...

Similarly, if the learner lacks either the facts, concepts, or principles related to biological classification
then these become the learning goals. The supportive
knowledge then forms the basis of the new learning
goal.

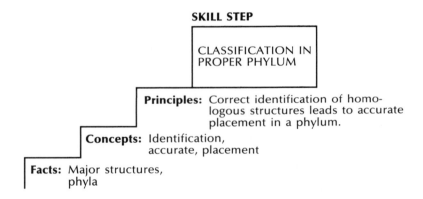

SKILL STEP

CLASSIFICATION IN
PROPER PHYLUM

Principles: Correct identification of homologous structures leads to accurate
placement in a phylum.

Concepts: Identification,
accurate, placement

Facts: Major structures,
phyla

...And Again

Goal-setting should define the learners' target levels of functioning for skills and knowledge. Both learners and teacher must have observable goals and objectives that both will know have been achieved. Thus, both will be able to identify the point of exit from the learning experience. At this point, again use the task goal or skill objective for which you have developed your lesson plan and teaching methods. Develop goals for your skill steps and supportive knowledge depending upon your diagnosis of the learners' levels of functioning. Simply note the skill objective based upon the diagnosis of the individual learners' performances.

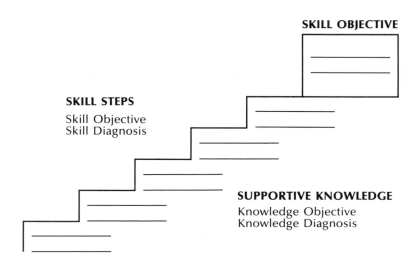

SKILL OBJECTIVE

SKILL STEPS
Skill Objective
Skill Diagnosis

SUPPORTIVE KNOWLEDGE
Knowledge Objective
Knowledge Diagnosis

Exercising Goal-Setting Skills

Developing Learning Programs

The purpose of the learning program is to help the learners to achieve the learning goals. Our diagnostic skills showed us where the learners are functioning. Our goal-setting skills showed us where the learners are going to learn to function. Now, our program development or programming skills are going to show us how to get there. Our programming skills enable us to develop and implement the skill steps toward achieving our skill objective. Each skill objective is broken down to an atomistic level, beginning with our learners' levels of functioning. This way, we insure that our learners can achieve the skill objective. Most importantly, our programming skills enable us to tailor the learning programs to the learners' unique needs. Again, the learners know where they are beginning, where they are going and how to get there. They have every assurance that they will achieve their objective, due to the systematic development of their learning programs. Thus, our programming skills facilitate the learners' essential movements through the action phase of learning: acting to get from where they are to where they want or need to be with the skills content. The learners can act to achieve their learning goals, and they can learn from the effectiveness of their actions how to modify future learning programs.

Learning Programs

The essential question of programming is: can we break down the steps to the skill objective so that the learners can perform them? The presentation is the primary phase when the teacher's programming skills are implemented. Our skill objectives were set based upon our diagnoses of the learners' performances. When the learners can analyze the learning experiences, then they can learn the responding skills comprising the task goal: responding to the learning experience.

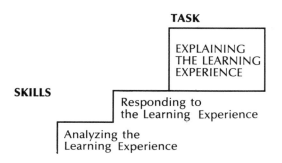

Developing the Skill Program

After we have set the skills goals, then, we must develop the skills steps to achieve the goals. For example, in teaching responding to the learning experience as our learning skill objective, we have set an immediate objective of responding to content. Now we must treat this skill step of responding to content as if it were a skill objective, and develop the subskill steps to achieve that objective.

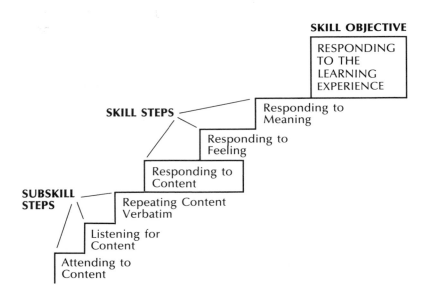

SKILL OBJECTIVE

RESPONDING TO THE LEARNING EXPERIENCE

SKILL STEPS

Responding to Meaning

Responding to Feeling

Responding to Content

SUBSKILL STEPS

Repeating Content Verbatim

Listening for Content

Attending to Content

Developing the Skill Steps

Upon the development of the skill steps, we may discover that there are certain facts and/or concepts and/or principles that the learner lacks. For example, we have now introduced the concept of responding as well as other facts and concepts. Perhaps we have to define responding: responding is defined by the interchangeability of expression. Thus, the learners will learn the supportive knowledge which they require to correctly perform the skill steps.

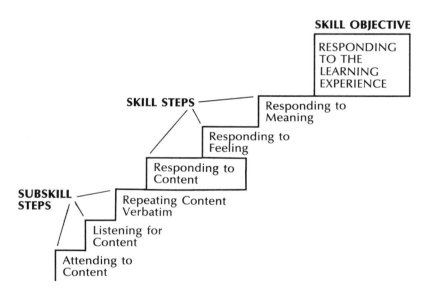

SKILL OBJECTIVE

RESPONDING TO THE LEARNING EXPERIENCE

SKILL STEPS
Responding to Meaning
Responding to Feeling
Responding to Content

SUBSKILL STEPS
Repeating Content Verbatim
Listening for Content
Attending to Content

Principles: If you respond to content, feeling and meaning you will have responded to the learning experience.
Concepts: Attending, listening, repeating, responding
Facts: Teacher, content, experience

Developing Supportive Knowledge

The skill steps provide a means for determining the exact level of learner performance. The supporting knowledge provides even greater detail to the performance of the learner. Thus the learning program can be developed and delivered efficiently and effectively.

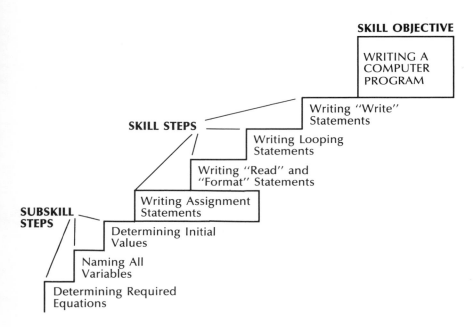

SKILL OBJECTIVE

WRITING A COMPUTER PROGRAM

SKILL STEPS

Writing "Write" Statements

Writing Looping Statements

Writing "Read" and "Format" Statements

Writing Assignment Statements

SUBSKILL STEPS

Determining Initial Values

Naming All Variables

Determining Required Equations

Principles: If you can write assignment, read, looping, and write statements, you can write a computer program.
Concepts: Assignments, write, read, looping
Facts: Statements, computer program

Repeating Again...

The following example details the skill steps, skill objectives and supportive information required to identify major homologous structures.

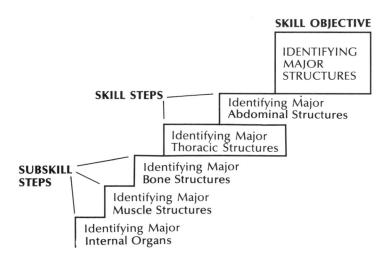

SKILL OBJECTIVE

IDENTIFYING MAJOR STRUCTURES

SKILL STEPS

Identifying Major Abdominal Structures

Identifying Major Thoracic Structures

SUBSKILL STEPS

Identifying Major Bone Structures

Identifying Major Muscle Structures

Identifying Major Internal Organs

Principles: If major structures are identified, proper classification is possible.
Concepts: Classification, homology
Facts: Frog, structures, phyla

...And Again

Our programming develops the skill steps and knowledge which the learners require in order to achieve the skill objective. Based upon the diagnosis of the learners' levels of functioning, the learning program provides all of the skills and knowledge required to achieve the skill objective. The learners have atomistic programs that lead them to their learning goals. At this point, refer again to the skill objective for which you have developed your lesson plan. Develop the skill steps and knowledge for your learners based upon their unique objectives.

Principles: _____

Concepts: _____

Facts: _____

Exercising Programming

Monitoring Learner Performance

The purpose of the monitoring program is to observe the feedback from the learners' performances. Once the learners have acted on the program to achieve the learning objective, they receive feedback from their actions. The purpose of the monitoring is to assess this feedback. The monitoring skills enable us to assess the applications the learners have made of the skills they have supposedly acquired. In other words, the monitoring skills assess the skills application in a real-life context. That, after all, is what the teaching and learning process is all about. Our learners have acted upon their learning programs. They are attempting to apply the skills they have acquired. Monitoring skills will allow us to assess the effectiveness of this application. Accordingly, the exercise and summary phases will be the most effective times for the teacher to use the monitoring skills. In so doing, our monitoring skills will serve to facilitate a recycling of learning. The learners have acted by attempting to perform the skill, and will now receive feedback from their actions. This feedback will serve to stimulate more extensive exploration of where the learners now are in relation to learning: thus, obtaining a more accurate understanding of where they now want or need to be; and therefore, determining more effective action to help them learn to perform the skill correctly.

The first application of monitoring is to observe skill performance. The discrimination to be made here is simply whether or not the learners have applied the skills. If the skill has been performed, then the learner is giving evidence of readiness for the next learning experience. If the skill has not been performed, then the learner must recycle the learning experience. For example, monitoring will determine whether or not the learner has responded to the content as preparation for learning to respond to the learning experience. This recycling requires new learning goals to be set and new programming to be done, in order to achieve this subgoal.

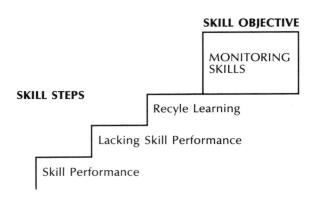

Monitoring Skill Performance

The second use of monitoring is to determine the performance level of the skill steps. If the skill has not been performed, then the skill steps must become the next learning process. For example, the learner may be able to attend and listen to the content, but unable to repeat it verbatim. This new diagnosis facilitates the learner's new explorations of where he or she is with the skill. It requires a new goal to be set, i.e., repeating the content verbatim, to facilitate the learner's more accurate understanding of where he or she wants or needs to be with the skill. A new program must be developed to initiate more effective action towards the achievement of this subgoal.

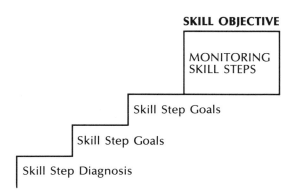

Monitoring Skill Steps

The third use of monitoring is to check the level of supportive knowledge available to the learner. If a skill step cannot be performed, then the supportive knowledge must be assessed in a recycling of the learning process. For example, if the learner cannot repeat the content verbatim, it may be because the learner lacks some level of supportive knowledge. Perhaps the learner cannot comprehend the concept of verbatim repetition. Knowledge of this principle becomes a goal, and a learning program can be developed to achieve the goal.

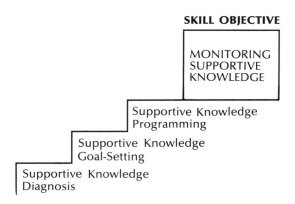

SKILL OBJECTIVE

MONITORING
SUPPORTIVE
KNOWLEDGE

Supportive Knowledge
Programming

Supportive Knowledge
Goal-Setting

Supportive Knowledge
Diagnosis

Monitoring Supportive Knowledge

For example, learners may not be able to determine the initial values of variables in a computer program because they lack the principle that if all variables are initialized to zero at the beginning of the program then error "debugging" is simplified. Knowledge of this principle becomes a learning goal. Thus, the supportive knowledge available must be monitored to determine the essential steps to insure success of the learning program.

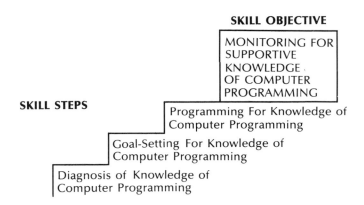

SKILL OBJECTIVE

MONITORING FOR SUPPORTIVE KNOWLEDGE OF COMPUTER PROGRAMMING

SKILL STEPS

Programming For Knowledge of Computer Programming

Goal-Setting For Knowledge of Computer Programming

Diagnosis of Knowledge of Computer Programming

Repeating Again...

The essential point is that every break-down of the curriculum into atomistic steps allows an intervention process to be generated based upon proper learner diagnosis. Thus, monitoring provides the feedback essential to the goal-setting process for the next learning program.

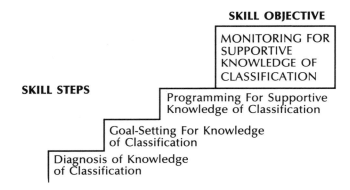

SKILL OBJECTIVE

MONITORING FOR
SUPPORTIVE
KNOWLEDGE OF
CLASSIFICATION

SKILL STEPS

Programming For Supportive
Knowledge of Classification

Goal-Setting For Knowledge
of Classification

Diagnosis of Knowledge
of Classification

...And Again

Our monitoring skills enable us to assess the performance of skills and to recycle the learner into a new learning experience; or, to recycle the learner through select dimensions of the same or similar learning experience. If the learner fails to apply the skill correctly, then the learning process is recycled. The level of skill steps and supportive knowledge are diagnosed in order to help the learner explore where he or she wants or needs to be. Programs are developed to help the learner get there. At this point, use the skill objective for which you have developed your lesson plan again. Make certain you are prepared to monitor the skill application in order to determine whether to cycle the learner into a new learning experience, or recycle the learner through the same learning experience.

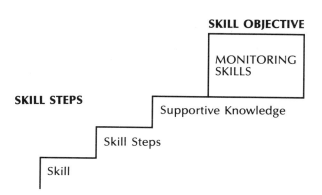

Exercising Monitoring

Exercising

Again, we employ our teaching delivery skills to facilitate the learners' movements through E-U-A. We can use our CPS for making all teaching deliveries when "thinking on our feet," in or out of the classroom. We can apply the CPS skills in any critical situation that involves teaching and learning. For example, we can use our teaching delivery skills in communicating at home with our spouses or friends. Or we could use them in communicating with superiors or subordinates at work. We could also teach our learners the basic CPS skills so that they would be able to diagnose, set goals, program and monitor their own performance.

SKILL OBJECTIVE:	Learners will discriminate levels of performance by learning teaching delivery skills under classroom conditions at a 90% level of accurate discriminations.
DIAGNOSE:	Skills, steps, knowledge
SET GOALS:	Skills, steps, knowledge
PROGRAM:	Skills, steps, knowledge
MONITOR:	Skills, steps, knowledge

Exercising CPS

You may wish to repeat CPS exercises. Apply the teaching delivery skills objective to the living or working contexts. Develop your diagnoses, goals, programs and monitoring skills program.

SKILL OBJECTIVE: _____

_____

DIAGNOSE: _____

SET GOALS: _____

PROGRAM: _____

MONITOR: _____

Repeating CPS

Try to make a variety of living, learning and working CPS applications with your specialty skills content.

_____

_____

_____

_____

_____

_____

_____

_____

_____

_____

_____

Applying CPS

Summarizing

Perhaps you will again outline your CPS for teaching your specialty skill content. Simply outline the delivery processes by which you would facilitate the achievement of your skill objective.

_____

_____

_____

_____

_____

If you are able to outline your CPS, then we are pleased because we have accomplished our training skill objective:

> The teachers will make teaching deliveries by implementing content processing skills under formal and informal conditions at levels that facilitate the learners' process movements.

Indexing CPS

You will also be happy if you have accomplished our CPS training skill objective: you are now capable of making a teaching delivery in your specialty skills content. You can make a teaching delivery in any area where you have conquered the content.

PHASES OF LEARNING

	PRE-LEARNING	I	II	III
TEACHER:				
CPS	PREPARING	DIAGNOSING	GOAL-SETTING	PROGRAMMING
	Content	Skills	Skills	Skills
	Organization	Steps	Steps	Steps
	Methods	Knowledge	Knowledge	Knowledge

LEARNER: INVOLVING ▶EXPLORING   UNDERSTANDING   ACTING
MONITORING SKILLS

Summarizing CPS

Our expertise in our CPS is what enables us to develop teaching and learning programs. Because our content is developed and organized around skills, we are able to program every learner's experience. Each learner becomes a unique entity, with his or her own unique starting point for learning. Effective teachers teach learners, and we are effective teachers. We teach content to learners. Our teaching delivery is totally dependent upon moment-to-moment diagnosis of the learners' performances. We do not take still and static photos of living and learning. We take continuous and on-going motion pictures of the learner in interaction with the content. These motion pictures enable every learner to succeed in every learning effort. Our learners cannot fail, because they begin where they are, and move to where they can go. They cannot fail because they are learning. Our teaching delivery skills are based upon the moment-to-moment relationships of the learners with the content. They are also based upon the moment-to-moment relationship of the teacher with the learners. This is the topic of the next chapter.

References

Berenson, D. H., Berenson, S. R. and Carkhuff, R. R. *The Skills of Teaching—Content Development Skills.* Amherst, MA: Human Resource Development Press, 1978.(a)

Berenson, D. H., Berenson, S. R. and Carkhuff, R. R. *The Skills of Teaching—Lesson Planning Skills. Amherst, MA: Human Resource Development Press, 1978.(b)*

Carkhuff, R. R. and Berenson, D. H. *The Skilled Teacher.* Amherst, MA: Human Resource Development Press, 1981.

Clark, D. C. "Teaching Concepts in the Classroom," *Journal of Educational Psychology,* 1971, *62,* 253–278.

Flanders, N. A. "Diagnosing and Utilizing Social Structures in Classroom Learning," in *The Dynamics of Instructional Groups.* National Society for the Study of Education, 59th Yearbook, Part II. Chicago, IL: University of Chicago Press, 1960.

Flanders, N. A. "Teacher Influence in the Classroom: Research on Classroom Climate," in *Theory and Research in Teaching.* A Bellack, ed. New York, NY: Columbia Teacher's College, 1963.

Hudgins, B. B. *Self-Contained Training Materials for Teacher Education.* Bloomington, IN: National Center for the Development of Training Materials in Teaching Education, Indiana University, 1974.

Kaya, E., Gerhard, M., Staslewski, A. and Berenson, D. H. *Developing a Theory of Educational Practices for the Elementary School.* Norwalk, CT: Ford Foundation Fund for the Improvement of Education, 1967.

Pfeiffer, Isobel L. "Teaching in Ability-Grouped English Classes: A Study of Verbal Interaction and Cognitive Goals," *Journal of Teacher Education,* 1966, *17,* No. 3.

4.
Interpersonal Processing Skills

Perhaps the most important set of skills that any one human being can have is the ability to relate to another human being. The most effective way of relating is to process interpersonally with that other human: to facilitate exploring, understanding, and acting of the other person. The active ingredients that serve to facilitate or retard human relationships and human development are interpersonal. Depending upon the level of concession by the learners, the teachers may have dramatically constructive or destructive effects upon the learners. Interpersonal skills enable a person to "walk in another's moccasins": to see the world through the other's eyes and communicate what is seen; to assist the other person in processing to surmount the problems and achieve the goals. Interpersonal processing skills (IPS) emphasize the internal frames of reference of the learners as they move through learning. These skills enable the teacher to relate the learners' frames of reference to the teaching goals. They are the catalysts that activate the learners to receive all other teaching ingredients.

Interpersonal Delivery

A number of studies have shown that the teachers' interpersonal skills relate to the learners' academic as well as social achievement. Perhaps the most illuminating study of interpersonal teaching skills was conducted by Aspy and Roebuck (1977). They offered third grade reading teachers three feeling-word cards to use in responding to the learners after recitation. Thus, the teachers responded: "You feel happy because you did so well," "You feel sad because you missed that part," "You feel angry because you still can't get that word." Reading achievement improved significantly because the teachers responded to the learners' frames of reference instead of making the more conventional response, "Next!" In particular, these interpersonal skills can be summarized as attending or paying attention (Carkhuff, 1983; Carkhuff and Berenson, 1981); responding or being empathic with the learners' frames of reference (Aspy, 1972; Aspy and Roebuck, 1977; Bloom, et al, 1956; Carkhuff, 1969, 1971; Flanders, 1970); personalizing or being additive in understanding the learners' problems or goals (Carkhuff, 1983; Carkhuff and Berenson, 1981); individualizing or initiating programs to meet the learners' unique needs (Carkhuff, 1983; Carkhuff and Berenson, 1981); and reinforcing the learners from their own internal frames of reference (Aspy and Roebuck, 1977; Gage, 1977). The basic principle of interpersonal skills is that all productive learning begins with the learners' frames of reference.

Principles of Interpersonal Skills

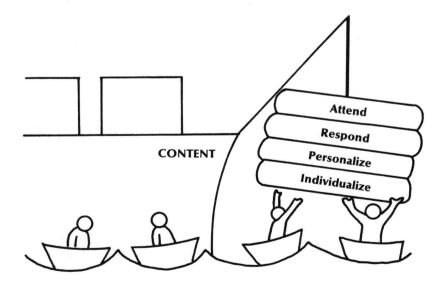

CONTENT

Attend
Respond
Personalize
Individualize

Interpersonal Delivery Skills

Our IPS teaching objective in this lesson is as follows:

> *The teachers will make teaching deliveries by implementing interpersonal processing skills under formal and informal conditions and at levels that facilitate the learners' process movements.*

Before you learn interpersonal processing skills, you may want an index of your skills in this area. Perhaps you can take some teaching objective in your specialty content and outline the interpersonal processes by which you would facilitate its achievement.

_____

_____

_____

_____

_____

Indexing IPS

You will be happy if you emphasized relating to the learners' frames of reference. These IPS will include attending to the learners; responding to the learners' frames of reference; personalizing the learners' goals; individualizing the learners' programs; and monitoring the learning programs.

ATTENDING:	To the learners in order to involve them in learning.
RESPONDING:	To the learners in order to facilitate their exploring.
PERSONALIZING:	The learners' experiences in order to facilitate their understanding.
INDIVIDUALIZING:	Programs in order to facilitate learner acting.
REINFORCING:	The learning in order to facilitate learner recycling.

PHASES OF LEARNING

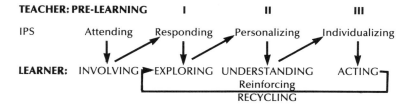

Overviewing IPS

Attending to the Learners

We prepare for our teaching delivery by attending to
our learners. Attending means being attentive or paying attention to our learners; it means that we care
about what happens to them. We poise ourselves to
cover the learners with a "hovering attentiveness" just
as we do with an infant. When we provide our learners
with our full and undivided attention, we are initiating
the principle of reciprocal effect: the learners give us,
in return, their full and undivided attention. The
learners give us the input which we need to initiate the
teaching delivery process. Attending involves the
learners in the learning process. By attending to the
learners we communicate an interest in their welfare.
We also receive input and feedback concerning the effectiveness of the learning experience from the things
we see and hear our learners do and say.

Attending

Attending physically means that we posture ourselves in such a way as to give our learners our full and undivided attention. It means that we are "with them." It is precisely this type of attention that we expect from our learners with regard to the learning experience. As was covered in the initial stages of our learning skills program, we now use precisely the same skill steps that our learners employed. For example, in relation to our class or groups of learners, we position ourselves at the vertex of a right angle incorporating both extreme perimeters of the learners in our classroom. Similarly, we lean forward or toward our learners, just as we do with all things in which we are interested. Finally, we make frequent eye contact with all of our learners.

Practice these attending skills in groups of two or three. What other ways can you attend to your learners?

We attend to our learners in their absence when we develop and organize our content. We attend to our learners in their presence when we posture ourselves to attend physically to them, observe them, and listen to them. All these attending skills serve to involve the learner in the learning process.

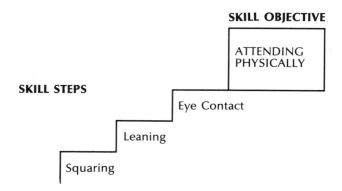

Attending Physically to the Learners

Observing means being able to "see" the appearance and behavior of learners, which give you clues to their experience: instead of a crowd of youthful faces, you see a frown, a grin, a pair of eyes that follow you in bright anticipation. One way of observing both appearance and behavior is for us to watch the skills in attending physically. That is, we observe the learners' squaring, leaning, and eyeing behaviors. We can make inferences from these cues. Physically, we can infer whether the learners have high, moderate or low levels of energy. Emotionally and interpersonally, we can infer whether they are "up," neutral or "down." Intellectually, we can infer whether they have a high, moderate or low level of readiness for learning.

Practice these observing skills in groups of two or three. What other dimensions can you observe in your learners?

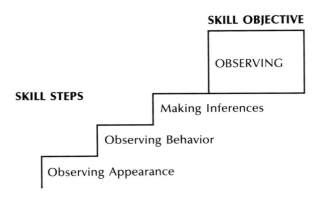

Observing the Learners

Listening means being able to "hear" what has been said, and how it has been said, in order to understand the learners' experiences. Instead of a babble of voices, we pick out this learner's calm and assured comment, or another's hesitant and embarrassed question. The skill steps involved in listening include at least the following: suspending our own judgments, i.e., not listening to ourselves; resisting all distractions in order to focus upon the expression of the learners; and recalling the content of the learners' verbal expressions. These skill steps will insure that we have at least heard the content of the learners' expressions.

Practice repeating verbatim the content of the learners' expressions. What other dimensions are involved in listening?

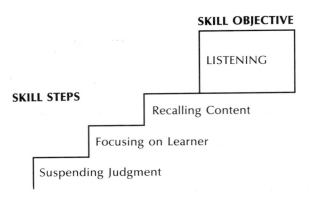

Listening to the Learners

In summary, our attending skills involve at least three skill objectives: attending physically in order to pay attention to the learners; observing in order to "see" the learners; and listening, in order to "hear" the learners. In addition, attending physically prepares us for observing, and observing prepares us for listening. These attending skills, when employed simultaneously, will converge to involve the learners in the learning process. At this point, you will want to practice using these skills simultaneously. First, practice attending physically, observing and listening with people, like yourselves, who are committed to teaching skills. Then apply these skills in your classrooms with your learners. You are sure to find the principle of reciprocal effect in operation: the learners will attend constructively to you to the same degree that you attend constructively to them.

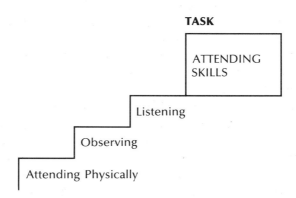

TASK

ATTENDING SKILLS

Listening

Observing

Attending Physically

Exercising Attending

Responding to the Learners

Responding is the key interpersonal ingredient. Responding means communicating an understanding of the experiences expressed by the learners. Responding means that we empathically enter the experiences of the learners—sit in their seats, see the experiences through their eyes—and communicate to them our understanding of those experiences. When we respond to the learners' experiences we are accomplishing two essential teaching purposes: 1) we are coming into contact with the learners' frames of reference; and 2) we are bringing the learners into contact with their own frames of reference. Again, the most fundamental principle of learning is that all learning begins with the learners' frames of reference. Our responsiveness is the way we enter the learners' experiences and communicate to them our understanding of their points of view. Responding initiates the first phase of learning. After involving the learners in the learning process through attending, we now facilitate their exploration through responding. Responding skills are employed simultaneously with the diagnostic delivery skills to facilitate the learners' explorations. The responding skills serve to allow us to enter the learners' internal frames of reference. The diagnostic skills serve to assess the learners from an external—the teacher's—frame of reference. Both the responding and the diagnostic skills converge to facilitate the learners' explorations of where they are in the learning experience. The point at which the learners begin their learning program is now clear to both teacher and learners, from both an internal and external frame of reference.

Responding

The first way of responding to our learners is to communicate our understanding of the content they are expressing. We can capture the content of an expression by repeating it verbatim. With more lengthy expressions, we can repeat the gist or the common theme. For example, one of the learners might say the following:

"Those tests are always like that. They don't test what you know."

When responding to content, we can recall the content by repeating the expression verbatim to ourselves. Then we can communicate our grasp of the content by reflecting the gist of it to the learners, using the reflective format, "You're saying _____." For example, we might respond to the content in the above expression as follows:

"You're saying that the tests don't test what you know."

Practice capturing the common themes of learners in small training groups. Assign one person the role of teacher-trainer, another the role of teacher, and have the rest be learners. Then rotate the roles until each has had the opportunity to be the teacher. Have the teacher attempt to capture the gist of the content of the learners' expressions using the reflective format, "You're saying _____," or some other format that helps you to paraphrase the content.

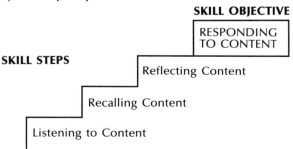

SKILL OBJECTIVE

RESPONDING TO CONTENT

SKILL STEPS

Reflecting Content

Recalling Content

Listening to Content

Responding to Content

The second way of responding to our learners is to communicate our understanding of the learners' feelings about their experiences. Both teachers and learners are often reluctant to enter the realm of feelings. This is largely because teachers have not been taught to do so, and when they try they are often inaccurate and thus ineffective. They tend to introduce their own feelings prematurely and out of context. Thus, teachers say things like "you shouldn't feel that way," or "that's not the way it is," long before they have given the learners a chance to explore. We can capture the feelings of an experience by doing three simple things: 1) repeating the expression verbatim to ourselves just as the learners expressed themselves to us; 2) asking ourselves, as if we were learners, "How does that make me feel?"; and 3) using the reflective format for communicating the feeling, i.e., "You feel _____."

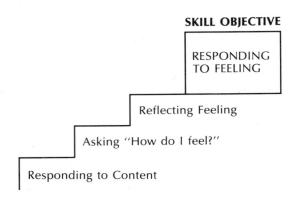

SKILL OBJECTIVE

RESPONDING
TO FEELING

Reflecting Feeling

Asking "How do I feel?"

Responding to Content

Responding to Feeling

For example, with the learners who stated that the tests did not test what they knew, the teacher might respond as follows: "You feel upset." One word of caution to teachers: often teachers do not use feeling words when they attempt to respond to their learners' experiences. Following is the beginning of a list of basic categories of feelings at strong, mild and weak levels of intensity. Use your training groups to practice responding to feeling, and to expand your repertoires of feeling words for application in your classrooms.

_____

_____

_____

_____

_____

_____

_____

_____

_____

_____

Expanding Feeling Words

CATEGORIES OF FEELINGS

LEVELS OF INTENSITY	CONFUSED	STRONG	WEAK	HAPPY	SAD	ANGRY	SCARED
Strong	Bewildered Trapped Troubled	Potent Super Powerful	Overwhelmed Impotent Small	Excited Elated Overjoyed	Hopeless Sorrowful Depressed	Furious Seething Enraged	Fearful Panicky Afraid
Mild	Disorganized Mixed-Up Foggy	Energetic Confident Capable	Incapable Helpless Insecure	Cheerful Up Good	Upset Distressed Down	Annoyed Frustrated Agitated	Threatened Insecure Uneasy
Weak	Bothered Uncomfortable Undecided	Sure Secure Durable	Shaky Unsure Soft	Glad Content Satisfied	Sorry Lost Bad	Uptight Dismayed Put Out	Timid Unsure Nervous

"Somehow," you may say, "the response to feeling seems incomplete."

"You're feeling confused because the response seems incomplete," is the response to make to such an expression.

Right on! The response to the learners' experience is incomplete without the meaning or the reason for the feeling. The response to feeling must be complemented by the reason for the feeling.

To develop our response to meaning we need only to: 1) build upon our feeling response; and 2) draw upon the content of the expression, asking ourselves the reason for the feeling. It remains only to use the reflective format to respond to the feeling and meaning, "You feel _____ because _____."

For example, we might formulate the following response to the learners who stated that tests didn't test what they knew: "You feel upset because the tests don't reflect what you know." This is a complete response to the learners' experience. It captures the feeling and the meaning.

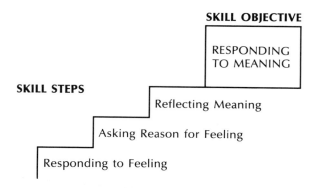

SKILL OBJECTIVE

RESPONDING TO MEANING

SKILL STEPS

Reflecting Meaning

Asking Reason for Feeling

Responding to Feeling

Responding to Meaning

In summary, our responding skills involve at least three objectives: responding to the content of the learners' expressions; responding to the feeling of the learners' experiences; and responding to the meaning of the learners' experiences. Each response prepares us for the next response. The responses to feeling and meaning culminate in our response to the learners' experiences. Responding accurately means that we are interchangeable in our understanding of the learners' frames of reference. By so doing, we have facilitated the learners' explorations of where they are in relation to their learning experiences. At this point, you will want to practice using all of your responsive skills simultaneously. As is appropriate, you can respond to the content, feeling or meaning of the learners' experience. Practice these skills in training groups, then apply these skills in your classrooms.

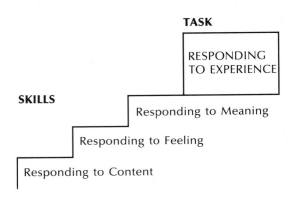

Exercising Responding

Personalizing the Learning Experience

Personalizing provides the transition from exploration to individualized action programs. Personalizing means individualizing the goals of learning. Personalizing means that we enter the learners' perceptions in order to develop goals that come from their frames of reference. When we personalize the learners' understanding of their experience, we accomplish two essential teaching purposes: 1) we relate the learners' frames of reference to learning goals; and 2) we establish individualized goals that will guide the development of our individualized learning programs. Our personalizing skills will enable us to extend the learners' frames of reference into goals that have value for the learners. Our personalizing skills will allow us to develop learning programs that will enable our learners to achieve their learning objectives. Personalizing introduces the second phase of learning. After responding to the learners' experiences in order to facilitate their exploration of where they are, we now personalize their understanding of their experiences. Personalizing helps the learners to understand where they are in relation to where they want or need to be in their learning experiences. Personalizing skills are used simultaneously with our goal-setting skills to facilitate the learners' understanding. The personalizing skills serve to extend the learners' internal frames of reference to an understanding of the externally derived goals. Both the personalizing and goal-setting skills converge to facilitate the learners' understanding of where they want or need to be in the learning experience. The goal of the learning program is therefore clear to teacher and learners from both an external, diagnostic frame of reference and also the learners' internal frames of reference.

Personalizing

When we responded to the experience of the learners, we did so at the level the learners themselves expressed. We attempted to respond interchangeably with the feeling and meaning of their experiences. In so doing, we allowed the learners to externalize the meanings or the reasons for the feelings. We accepted the learners at the level they presented themselves. Now we are going to go beyond the learners' presentations. We go beyond the learners' presentations by personalizing the meaning for the learners, through developing the implications of the experience for the learners. In so doing, we internalize the learners' responsibility for the experience. For example, we responded to the meaning of the learners' experience when we said, "You feel upset because the tests don't reflect what you know." Now we ask a question concerning the personal implications for the learner: "What are the implications of the experience for me?" Foremost among the implications is the fact that the learner did not do well on the test. It remains only to communicate this internalized meaning with the format: "You feel _____ because you _____." Thus, to continue this example, we may personalize our response to meaning as follows: "You feel upset because you didn't do well on the test." Practice making personalized responses to meaning in small training groups, rotating the roles among trainer, teacher, and learners.

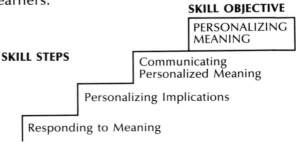

SKILL OBJECTIVE

PERSONALIZING MEANING

SKILL STEPS

Communicating Personalized Meaning

Personalizing Implications

Responding to Meaning

Personalizing the Meaning

Having personalized and internalized the meaning of the learner's experience, we now want to personalize the problem. After all, the learner's problem with the learning experience is an obstacle to learning. We can personalize the problem by developing the learner's deficit in the learning experience. As if we were the learner, we ask the question, "What is it that I lack that led to this experience?" For example, we personalized the meaning of the learner's experience with our response, "You feel upset because you didn't do well on the test?" Now, we answer the deficit question for the learner: the learner lacks the ability to handle these tests effectively. It remains for us to communicate this response deficit with the format, "You feel _____ because you cannot _____." Thus, to continue the example, we may personalize the problem as follows: "You feel upset because you can't handle these tests." The response personalizes the problem for the learner. Practice making personalized responses to problems in small training groups, rotating the roles among trainer, teacher, and learners.

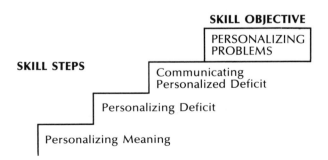

Personalizing the Problem

After personalizing the problem, we must personalize the feeling. Our learner now has a different per-
ception of the problem than he or she began with. The
meaning has changed. For one thing, the learner has
become accountable for his or her contribution to the
experience. And so, the feeling may change. We personalize the feeling the same way that we responded
to feeling. We ask the question, "How does that make
me feel?", just as if we were the learner. For example,
we personalized the learner's problem when we said:
"Your feel upset because you cannot handle the tests."
Now, we answer the new learning question for the
learner. Does the learner feel upset? Or does the
learner feel disappointed? All personalized feeling
responses conclude in disappointment in oneself. It remains for us to communicate this personalized feeling
with the same format as the personalized problem:
"You feel upset because you cannot handle the tests."
Thus, to continue the example, we can personalize the
feeling as follows: "You feel disappointed in yourself
because you cannot handle these tests." The response
personalizes the new feeling for the learner.

Practice making personalized feeling responses in
small training groups, rotating the roles among trainer,
teacher and learners.

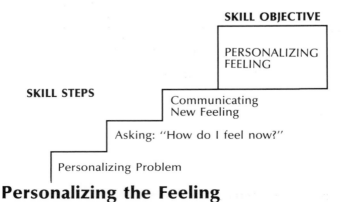

SKILL OBJECTIVE

PERSONALIZING
FEELING

SKILL STEPS

Communicating
New Feeling

Asking: "How do I feel now?"

Personalizing Problem

Personalizing the Feeling

Finally, we must personalize the goal. The problem, after all, dictates the goal. Indeed, the goal is simply the flip-side of the problem. The way we personalize the goal is simply to make explicit the goal that is implied by the personalized problem. For example, we personalized the learner's problem and feeling when we said: "You feel disappointed in yourself because you cannot handle these tests." Now we simply append an explicit statement of the goal. We do this by adding the goal statement: "...and you really want to." Thus, to continue our example, we may personalize the goal as follows: "You feel disappointed in yourself because you cannot handle these tests and you really want to." Such a response is a personalized goal statement.

Practice making personalized goal responses in small training groups, rotating the roles among trainer, teacher, and learners.

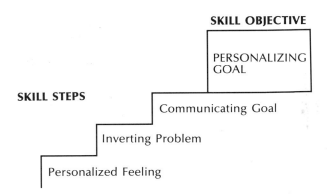

Personalizing the Goal

In summary, our personalizing goal skills involve at least four skill objectives: personalizing meaning; personalizing problems; personalizing feelings; and personalizing goals. Each personalized response prepares us for the next response, just as responding to feeling and meaning prepared us for personalizing. By personalizing the learners' goals, we have gone beyond the learners' expressions. We have facilitated the learners' understanding of where they are in relation to where they want to be in the learning experience.

At this point, you will want to practice using our personalizing skills. Only now, unlike responding, you will use these skills sequentially. You will lay a base of responsive skills that are interchangeable with our learners' expressions. Then, you will move sequentially through your personalizing skills. You should always be careful to check your accuracy with your interchangeable responses to feeling and meaning. After you have practiced these skills in training groups, then you can apply them in your classrooms.

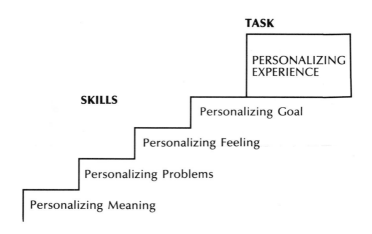

TASK

PERSONALIZING EXPERIENCE

SKILLS

Personalizing Goal

Personalizing Feeling

Personalizing Problems

Personalizing Meaning

Exercising Personalizing

Individualizing the Learners' Programs

The learning process culminates in an individualized action program. Individualizing means tailoring the learning programs to meet the learners' unique needs. Individualizing means entering each learner's perceptions in order to relate each program to that individualized frame of reference. When we individualize the learner's action program, we accomplish two essential teaching purposes: 1) we relate the learner's frame of reference to the learning programs; and 2) we relate the learner's frame of reference to individualized reinforcements for achievement in the learning programs. Our individualizing skills will enable us to help the learners to conclude the learning process. They will allow us to develop truly individualized learning programs that will enable our learners to achieve their learning objectives. Individualizing introduces the third phase of learning. Having personalized the learners' goals in order to facilitate their understanding of where they want or need to be, we now individualize their action programs to get there. Individualizing skills are used simultaneously with our programming skills to facilitate the learners' actions. The individualizing skills serve to extend the learners internal frames of reference to relate to the externally derived action programs. Both the individualizing and programming skills converge to facilitate the learners' acting to get from where they are to where they want or need to be. The steps of the learning program are clear to teacher and learners from both our external, diagnostic frames of reference and the learners' internal frames of reference.

Individualizing

When we personalized the goal for the learners, we captured their disappointment in their response deficits and transformed their problems into goal statements. It remains for us to individualize the learning goals. We individualize the learning goals by translating them into learning principles. Each learner can do this by developing an individualized learning principle that incorporates the skill to be learned, the particular application to be made and the unique human benefit to be achieved. To do this, we use the format for individualized learning principles: "If (skill), then (application) so that (benefit)." For example, we personalized the learning goal for our learner: "You feel disappointed in yourself because you cannot handle these tests and you really want to." Now we will individualize the learning goal with an individualized learning principle: "If I learn test-taking skills (skill), then I will be able to handle these testing situations (application), so that I can learn the subjects I need to pursue the career I choose." Such a response is an individualized learning goal statement. By achieving the skill, the learner can make the unique application and receive the unique benefit.

Practice making individualized learning goal statements in small training groups, rotating the roles among trainers, teacher, and learners.

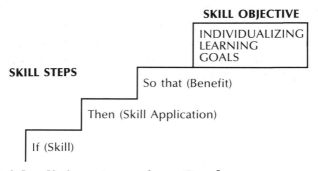

SKILL OBJECTIVE

INDIVIDUALIZING LEARNING GOALS

SKILL STEPS

So that (Benefit)

Then (Skill Application)

If (Skill)

Individualizing Learning Goals

Having an individualized learning goal statement allows us to individualize the sequencing of the learning. Most programs are comprised of steps that are sequenced contingently or by contingency where each step is dependent upon the performance of the previous step. Some learners cannot perform the steps as they are designed. They require programs individualized to their own particular learning or processing styles. The modes of individualizing include sequencing the steps from simple-to-complex, concrete-to-abstract and immediate-to-remote. Often these steps vary with those sequenced by contingency as well as with each other. For example, an interpersonal skills program could begin with facing another individual, a most simple step that can be performed readily. Or the same interpersonal skills program could begin with developing programs, the most concrete step. Or the same interpersonal skills program could begin by immediate experience.

Practice individualizing learning sequencing in small training groups. See how many more instances of difference in sequencing we may develop. These differences allow us to further individualize the learning programs.

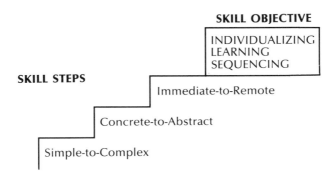

Individualizing Learning Sequencing

We can individualize the learning program even further by individualizing the learning steps. The learning steps emphasize what the learner has to do, know and feel. Perhaps the learner can perform two of these steps but not the third. The learner may be able to do the step but does not understand the supportive knowledge involved. Or the learner may be able to do and understand a step but has a negative attitude toward performing it. Test-taking skills, for example, may involve test preparation (doing), test concentration (knowing) and test relaxation (feeling) skill steps. Thus, to fully individualize learning steps we need to emphasize the learner's internalized learning steps in much the same manner that we developed the externalized steps.

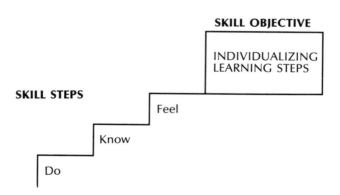

Individualizing Learning Steps

In summary, our individualizing learning skills involve at least three skill objectives: individualizing learning goals; individualizing learning sequencing; individualizing learning steps. Each individualized learning program prepares us for the next individualized learning program. By individualizing the learning programs, we have facilitated the learners' acting to get from where they are to where they want or need to be.

At this point, you may need to practice using your individualizing skills. Be careful to relate the internal frames of references of the learners to the external frames of reference of the content. After you have practiced these individualizing skills in training groups, then apply them in your classrooms.

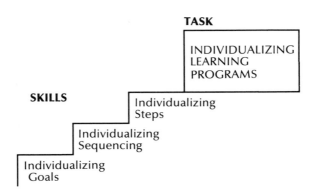

Exercising Individualizing

Reinforcing the Learners

We have developed an individualized learning program. We did this by putting together programs drawn from the learner's internalized and the teacher's externalized frames of reference. It only remains to reinforce the achievement of each step in the learning program. The reinforcement of learning flows directly from the learner's frame of reference just as did the individualized learning program. Indeed, the most potent reinforcement will be the long term benefits that will accrue to the learner by learning the skills. The potency of the teacher's reinforcement is related directly to the empathy of the teacher for the learner. Reinforcing serves to introduce the post-learning phase of recycling learning. Having individualized the learning programs to get the learners from where they are to where they want to be, we now individualize the reinforcements to get them there. Reinforcing skills are used simultaneously with our monitoring skills to stimulate the recycling of learning. The reinforcing skills serve to strengthen the skills applications that are monitored. The reinforcing skills also enhance the skill steps and supportive knowledge needed to acquire and apply the skill. Together, the reinforcing and monitoring skills insure the correct application of the skill requisite to the next cycle of learning.

Individualizing Reinforcement

The teacher uses his or her interpersonal skills to reinforce learning. The teacher simply makes a personalized response to learners' experiences based upon monitoring the skill application. In so doing, the teacher's task is to show the learners how learning each new skill, and making each new application, leads to the long-term benefit. Thus, the teacher personalizes the response by using the individualized learning principle:

"You feel _____ because you can (skill application) so that you are (benefit)."

Thus, for example, we might use the following positively reinforcing phrase with the learner in our illustration:

"You feel good because you are handling the tests so that you can move toward your career goals."

Such a response captures the feeling accompanying an effective skill application. It also complements the meaning of the skill application with the long-term benefit for the learner. This positively reinforcing response can also be used for the learning of skill steps and supportive knowledge, during either the cycling or recycling of learning.

Practice making positively reinforcing responses in small training groups, rotating the roles among trainer, teacher and learners.

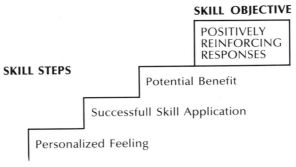

Reinforcing Positively

Obviously not all skill applications are satisfactorily discharged by all learners. Clearly, the teacher must use interpersonal skills to make a personalized response to the problems the learners are encountering. As with positive reinforcements, the teacher will use the skill application and benefits to make negatively reinforcing responses:

"You feel _____ because you cannot (skill application) so that you are not (benefit)."

Thus, for example, we might use the following negatively reinforcing phrase with the learner in our illustration:

"You feel bad because you cannot handle the tests and you are not moving toward your career goal."

Such a response captures the feeling and the problem of the learner's experience. At the same time, it does not punish the learner for his or her effort, however feeble. It puts the learning effort in the learner's hands by personalizing the response from the learner's frame of reference. This negatively reinforcing response can also be used for reinforcing learning skill steps and supportive knowledge.

Practice making negatively reinforcing responses in small training groups, rotating the roles among trainer, teacher, and learners.

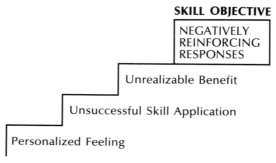

SKILL OBJECTIVE

NEGATIVELY REINFORCING RESPONSES

Unrealizable Benefit

Unsuccessful Skill Application

Personalized Feeling

Reinforcing Negatively

Finally, it is sometimes unclear to the teacher whether or not the learners are making effective skill applications. This is usually because the learner is not clear. It may require intense vigilance and fine discrimination on the teacher's part to make the determination. Ultimately, it must be determined before the learner moves on to new learning: either the learner has made the skill application or not. Accordingly, the teacher will either make a positively or negatively reinforcing response. In any event, the teacher can use the interpersonal skills to respond to the learner's experience at the moment.

"You feel _____ because sometimes you can and sometimes you cannot (skill application) so that you are not clear about (benefits)."

Thus, in the illustration, we might respond to the learner's mixed experience:

"You feel confused because you are handling some testing situations and not others, so that you are not clear about your movement toward your career goals."

Such a response comes from the learner's frame of reference, yet allows the teacher time to observe the learner's performance. It can also be employed for the learning of skill steps and supportive knowledge.

Practice making vigilant responses in small training groups, rotating the different participants in different roles.

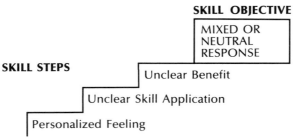

Being Vigilant

In summary, our individualized reinforcing skills involve at least three skill objectives: positively reinforcing responses; negatively reinforcing responses; and mixed or neutral responses. Each reinforcing response comes from the learner's own unique frame of reference. It incorporates the learner's feeling experience, skill application, and benefit.

At this point, practice using your reinforcing skills. Always emphasize observing the learner's performance vigilantly, in order to determine whether it is moving him or her toward or away from the skill application and the human benefit. After you have practiced these reinforcing skills in training groups, then you will want to apply them in your classrooms.

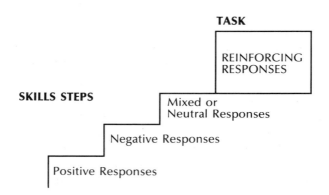

Exercising Reinforcing

Exercising

Again, we employ our interpersonal processing skills to facilitate the learners' movements through E-U-A. We can use IPS for facilitating all learning when "thinking on our feet," in or out of the classroom. We can apply the IPS skills in any critical situation that involves human relations in general, i.e., at home, school, or work. We can also teach our learners the basic IPS skills so that they can relate to others in facilitating their own and others' learning experiences.

SKILL OBJECTIVE:	Learners will communicate interpersonally by learning interpersonal processing skills under classroom conditions at effective levels of communication.
ATTENDING:	Skills, steps, knowledge
RESPONDING:	Skills, steps, knowledge
PERSONALIZING:	Skills, steps, knowledge
INDIVIDUALIZING:	Skills, steps, knowledge
REINFORCING:	Skills, steps, knowledge

Exercising IPS

You may wish to repeat interpersonal processing skills. Apply the interpersonal processing skills objectives to the living or working contexts. Develop your attending, responding, personalizing, individualizing and reinforcing skills programs.

SKILL OBJECTIVE: _____

_____

ATTENDING: _____

RESPONDING: _____

PERSONALIZING: _____

INDIVIDUALIZING: _____

REINFORCING: _____

Repeating IPS

Try to make a variety of living, learning and working interpersonal processing skills applications with our specialty skills content.

_____

_____

_____

_____

_____

_____

_____

_____

_____

_____

_____

Applying IPS

Summarizing

Perhaps you will again outline your use of interpersonal skills in teaching your specialty skill content. Simply outline the interpersonal process by which you would facilitate the achievement of your skill objective.

_____

_____

_____

_____

_____

If you are able to outline your interpersonal processing skills, then we are delighted because we have achieved our training skill objective:

> *The teachers will make teaching deliveries by implementing interpersonal processing skills under formal and informal conditions and at levels that facilitate the learners' process movements.*

Indexing IPS

You will also be happy if you have accomplished your IPS training skill objective: you are now capable of using your interpersonal skills in your specialty skills content. You can use your interpersonal processing skills in any area where you have conquered the content.

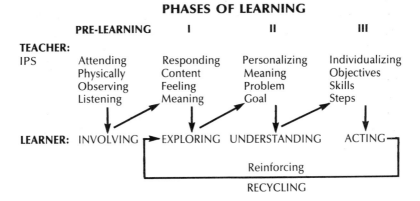

PHASES OF LEARNING

	PRE-LEARNING	I	II	III
TEACHER:				
IPS	Attending	Responding	Personalizing	Individualizing
	Physically	Content	Meaning	Objectives
	Observing	Feeling	Problem	Skills
	Listening	Meaning	Goal	Steps

LEARNER: INVOLVING → EXPLORING   UNDERSTANDING   ACTING

Reinforcing

RECYCLING

Summarizing IPS

In summary, interpersonal skills serve to engage the learners in the learning process: attending facilitates involvement; responding facilitates exploration; personalizing facilitates understanding; individualizing initiates action; and reinforcing recycles learning. Interpersonal skills offer a comprehensive approach to relating teachers to the students' frames of reference. In conclusion, interpersonal skills enable us to assess the learner/recipients' progress through the eyes of the learners themselves. In so doing, we can relate the learners' internal frames of reference to the external frame of the skills content. Thus, we can be guided by what is effective in helping the learners to move through the phases of learning. Our interpersonal skills enable us to converge objective reality with subjective experience.

References

Aspy, D. N. *Toward a Technology for Humanizing Education.* Champaign, IL: Research Press, 1972.

Aspy, D. N. and Roebuck, F. N. *KIDS Don't Learn from People They Don't Like.* Amherst, MA: Human Resource Development Press, 1977.

Bloom, B. S., Englehart, M. D., Furst, E. J., Hill, W. H. and Krathwohl, D. R. *A Taxonomy of Educational Objectives: Handbook I, The Cognitive Domain.* New York, NY: Longmans, Green, 1956.

Carkhuff, R. R. *Helping and Human Relations.* New York, NY: Holt, Rinehart & Winston, 1969.

Carkhuff, R. R. *The Development of Human Resources.* New York, NY: Holt, Rinehart & Winston, 1971.

Carkhuff, R. R. *The Art of Helping.* Amherst, MA: Human Resource Development Press, 1983.

Carkhuff, R. R. and Berenson, D. H. *The Skilled Teacher.* Amherst, MA: Human Resource Development Press, 1981.

Flanders, N. A. *Analyzing Teaching Behavior.* Reading, MA: Addison-Wesley, 1970.

Gage, N. L. *The Scientific Basis of the Art of Teaching.* New York, NY: Teachers College Press, 1977.

5.
Learning Management Skills

Learning management skills emphasize learner process-ing within the implementation of the teaching delivery plan. Thus, where appropriate, learners must explore, understand, and act upon their learning experience within each of the stages of the content organization, i.e., Review, Overview, Presentation, Exercise, and Sum-marize. The teacher employs content and interpersonal processing skills simultaneously to facilitate learner processing. Clearly, the better the teacher's content skills and knowledge, the more productive the content processing. Similarly, the better the teacher's repertoire of interpersonal responses, the more productive the in-terpersonal processing.

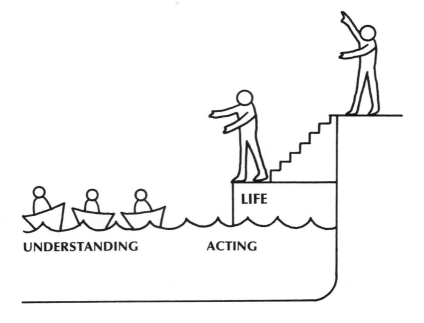

UNDERSTANDING   ACTING

LIFE

Learning Management

Learning management emphasizes learner processing within the teaching delivery. As such, learning management skills (LMS) emphasize three sets of skills. First, LMS emphasize the development of the teaching delivery plan which is organized around learner exercises and applications (Berenson, Berenson and Carkhuff, 1978; Berliner, 1977; Carkhuff and Berenson, 1981; French, et al., 1957; Gage, 1976, 1977; Kearney, 1953; Lumsdaine, 1964; Mager, 1962; Smith and Moore, 1962). Second, LMS emphasize the content processing skills that process the learners in terms of the requirements of the content (Berenson, Berenson and Carkhuff, 1979; Clark, 1971; Flanders, 1960, 1963; Hudgins, 1974; Kaya, Gerhard, Staslewski and Berenson, 1967; Pfeiffer, 1966). Finally LMS emphasize the interpersonal processing skills that process the content from the learners' frames of reference (Aspy, 1972; Aspy and Roebuck, 1977; Bloom, Englehart, Furst, Hill and Krathwohl, 1956; Carkhuff, 1969, 1971, 1983; Carkhuff, Berenson and Pierce, 1977; Flanders, 1970; Gage, 1977). Together, the content and interpersonal processing skills converge to facilitate learner processing within the stages of the teaching delivery plan.

Principles of Learning Management

Learning Management Skills

Our learning management skills training objective in this lesson is as follows:

The teachers will make teaching deliveries by implementing learning management skills under formal and informal conditions at levels that facilitate their learners' skill performances.

Before you learn learning management skills, you may want an index of your skills in this area. Perhaps you can take a teaching skill objective in your specialty content and outline how you would employ learning management skills to achieve this objective.

_____

_____

_____

_____

_____

Indexing LMS

You should be pleased if you emphasized processing within your teaching delivery plan. Thus, the teachers will use content processing skills (CPS) and interpersonal processing skills (IPS) to facilitate learner performance within each of the stages of the teaching delivery plan.

CONTENT ORGANIZATION

CS — Contingency Skills
SA — Skill Applications
SS — Skill Steps
SP — Skill Performance
L — Learner
T — Teacher

Overviewing LMS

Managing Learning in the Review

Teachers employ their learning management skills during the Review by processing both content and learners. Thus, teachers employ their CPS to process the requirements of the content. Also, they use their IPS to process the experiences of the learners. Teachers employ both CPS and IPS simultaneously to facilitate learner exploring, understanding, and acting.

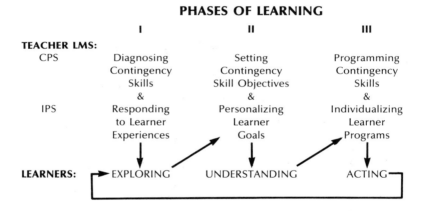

PHASES OF LEARNING

	I	II	III
TEACHER LMS:			
CPS	Diagnosing Contingency Skills	Setting Contingency Skill Objectives	Programming Contingency Skills
	&	&	&
IPS	Responding to Learner Experiences	Personalizing Learner Goals	Individualizing Learner Programs
LEARNERS:	EXPLORING	UNDERSTANDING	ACTING

Managing Learning in the Review

Thus, the teacher may diagnose the individual learners' performance or nonperformance of the contingency skills (CS) in the Review. The nonperforming learners are further diagnosed in terms of the skill step (SS) and/or supportive knowledge (SK) deficits. Objectives and programs may be developed and implemented accordingly until performance of the contingency skills is achieved. The learners who can perform the contingency skills proceed to the Overview.

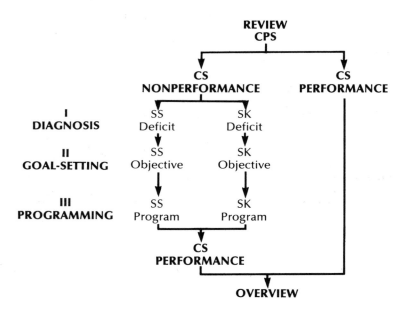

Content Processing in the Review

Simultaneously with the content processing, the teacher uses interpersonal skills to facilitate the processing of the learners' experiences. In general, the teacher may use a variation of generic responding, personalizing, and individualizing formats:

RESPONDING: "You feel (good or bad) because you (did or did not) perform the skill."

PERSONALIZING: "You feel (pleased or disappointed) because you (can or cannot) perform the skill and you are eager to (move on to the next skill or learn this skill)."

INDIVIDUALIZING: "If you learn to perform (skill), then you will be able to make (skill application) so that you will achieve (human benefit)."

Interpersonal Processing in the Review

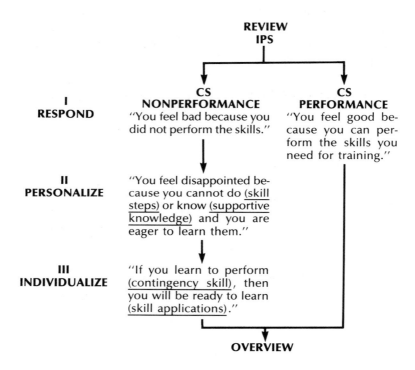

Interpersonal Processing in the Review

You many want to practice managing Review learning in your specialty content. Outline your teaching delivery plan for the Review. Indicate how you plan to use your learning management skills to implement your delivery plan.

REVIEW TEACHING DELIVERY PLAN:

_____

_____

_____

_____

_____

LEARNING MANAGEMENT SKILLS:

_____

_____

_____

_____

_____

Practicing LMS in the Review

Managing Learning in the Overview

Teachers continue to apply their learning management skills during the Overview by processing both the content and the learners' experiences. Thus, teachers employ their content and interpersonal processing skills simultaneously to facilitate learner exploring, understanding, and acting. At the same time, the teachers **tell-show-do** potential skill applications in order to motivate the learners to learn.

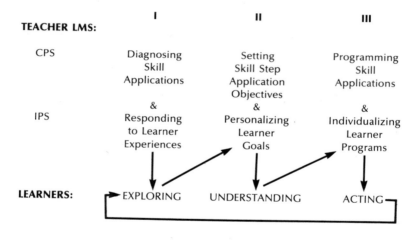

PHASES OF LEARNING

TEACHER LMS:	I	II	III
CPS	Diagnosing Skill Applications	Setting Skill Step Application Objectives	Programming Skill Applications
IPS	& Responding to Learner Experiences	& Personalizing Learner Goals	& Individualizing Learner Programs
LEARNERS:	EXPLORING	UNDERSTANDING	ACTING

Managing Learning in the Overview

The teacher may diagnose the individual learner's ability to illustrate a skill application (SA) during the Overview. Nonillustration elicits a further diagnosis focusing upon the deficits of contingency skills (CS) and/or images of skill application (SA). In turn, objectives are set and programs developed and implemented until skill applications are illustrated. The learners who can illustrate skill applications proceed to the Presentation.

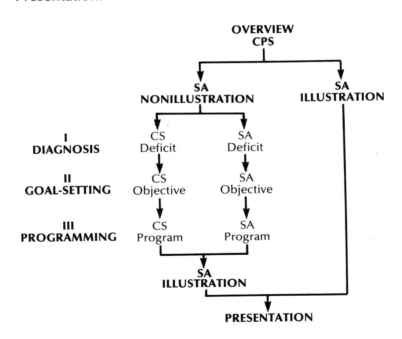

Content Processing in the Overview

Simultaneously, interpersonal processing is used to facilitate learning. The teacher responds to facilitate learner exploration of the Overview experiences, personalizes to facilitate learner understanding of the Overview goals, and individualizes to facilitate learner acting upon the Overview programs.

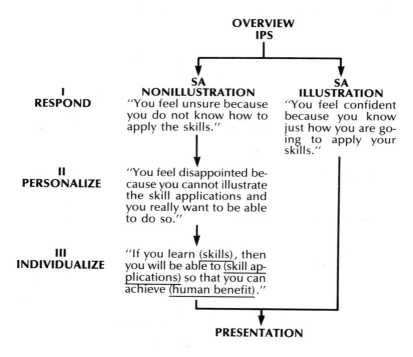

Interpersonal Processing in the Overview

You may want to practice managing Overview learning in your specialty content. Outline your teaching delivery plan for the Overview. Indicate how you plan to use your learning management skills to implement your delivery plan.

OVERVIEW TEACHING DELIVERY PLAN:

_____

_____

_____

_____

_____

LEARNING MANAGEMENT SKILLS:

_____

_____

_____

_____

_____

Practicing LMS in the Overview

Managing Learning in the Presentation

Learners use their learning management skills during the **doing** method of the Presentation. During the **tell** and **show** stages, the teachers emphasize their presentations while the learners **hear** and **see** the reception. During **do** stage, the teachers use their CPS and IPS to manage the learners' performances of the skills steps to be learned.

PHASES OF LEARNING

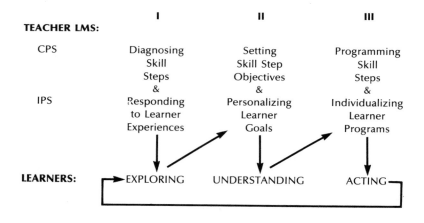

Managing Learning in the Presentation

The teacher diagnoses skill step (SS) performance during the presentation. When the skill steps are not performed, the teacher further analyzes the skill step and/or supportive knowledge (SK) deficits. Objectives are set and learning programs developed and implemented. The learners who can perform the skill steps proceed to the Exercise stage.

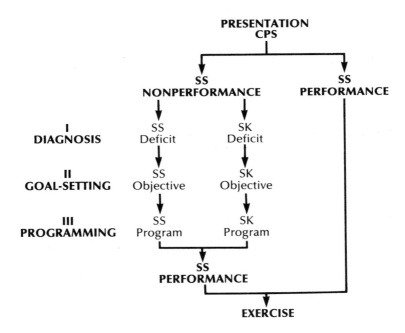

Content Processing in the Presentation

Simultaneously, the teacher uses interpersonal processing to facilitate learning in the Presentation by: responding to the learners' experiences, personalizing learning goals, and individualizing learning programs.

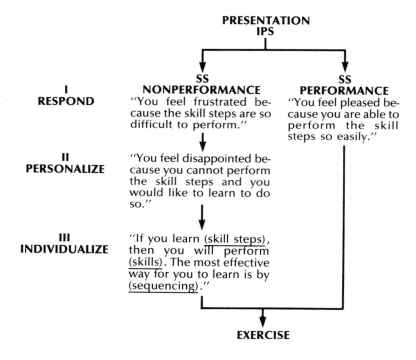

PRESENTATION
IPS

| I **RESPOND** | **SS NONPERFORMANCE** "You feel frustrated because the skill steps are so difficult to perform." | **SS PERFORMANCE** "You feel pleased because you are able to perform the skill steps so easily." |

| II **PERSONALIZE** | "You feel disappointed because you cannot perform the skill steps and you would like to learn to do so." |

| III **INDIVIDUALIZE** | "If you learn (skill steps), then you will perform (skills). The most effective way for you to learn is by (sequencing)." |

EXERCISE

Interpersonal Processing in the Presentation

You may want to practice Presentation learning in your specialty content. Outline your Presentation teaching delivery plan and indicate how you plan to use your learning management skills to implement it.

PRESENTATION TEACHING DELIVERY PLAN:

_____

_____

_____

_____

_____

LEARNING MANAGEMENT SKILLS:

_____

_____

_____

_____

_____

Practicing LMS in the Presentation

Managing Learning in the Exercise

During the Exercise stage of learning, the teachers manage learner learning exclusively. The emphasis is upon learner skill step performance. The teachers utilize all of their CPS and IPS to facilitate learner processing or performance of the skill steps during the Exercise.

PHASES OF LEARNING

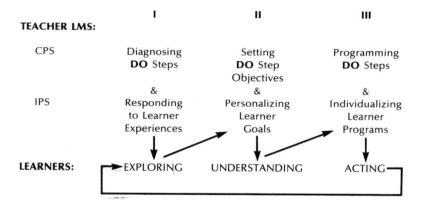

	I	II	III
TEACHER LMS:			
CPS	Diagnosing **DO** Steps	Setting **DO** Step Objectives	Programming **DO** Steps
IPS	& Responding to Learner Experiences	& Personalizing Learner Goals	& Individualizing Learner Programs
LEARNERS:	EXPLORING	UNDERSTANDING	ACTING

Managing Learning in the Exercise

The teacher further diagnoses skill step (SS) performance during the Exercise stage. The exercises provide an opportunity to further analyze **do** and/or **think** step deficits, set learning objectives, and develop learning programs. The learners who can perform the skill steps proceed to the Summary.

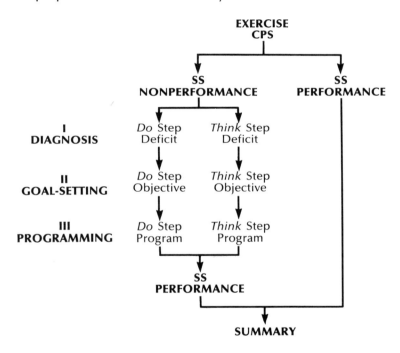

Content Processing in the Exercise

Simultaneously, the teacher will respond, personalize, and individualize to facilitate the learner's processing of skill steps during the Exercise.

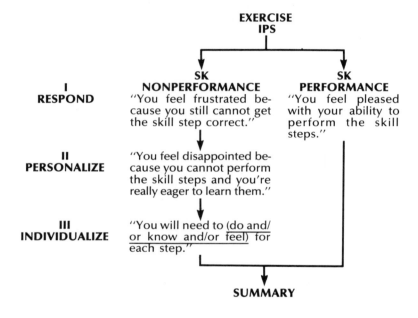

Interpersonal Processing in the Exercise

You may want to practice managing Exercise learning in your specialty content. Outline your teaching delivery plan for the Exercise. Indicate how you plan to use your learning management skills to implement your delivery plan.

EXERCISE TEACHING DELIVERY PLAN:

_____

_____

_____

_____

_____

LEARNING MANAGEMENT SKILLS:

_____

_____

_____

_____

_____

Practicing LMS in the Exercise

Managing Learning in the Summary

Teachers use their learning management skills in the Summary to facilitate learner processing of skill performance. Even during this post-learning stage, the learners may need to process their skill performance. Accordingly, the teachers use CPS and IPS simultaneously to facilitate learner exploring, understanding, and acting.

PHASES OF LEARNING

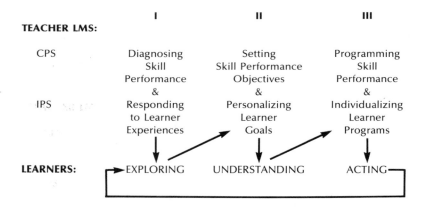

TEACHER LMS:	I	II	III
CPS	Diagnosing Skill Performance	Setting Skill Performance Objectives	Programming Skill Performance
	&	&	&
IPS	Responding to Learner Experiences	Personalizing Learner Goals	Individualizing Learner Programs
LEARNERS:	EXPLORING	UNDERSTANDING	ACTING

Finally, the teacher diagnoses skill performance during the Summary. Nonperformance requires further analysis of the skill step (SS) and/or supportive knowledge (SK) deficits, setting of skill step and/or supportive knowledge objectives, and development and implementation of skill step and/or supportive knowledge programs. Successful performance of the skills prepares the learners for real-life applications and transfers.

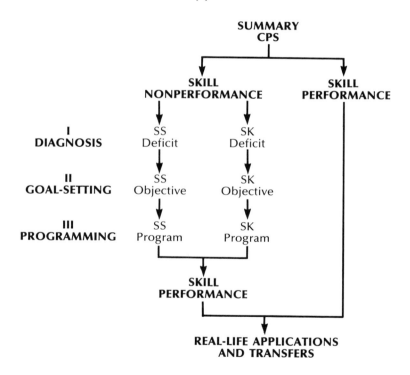

Content Processing in the Summary

Simultaneously, the teacher will respond, personalize, and individualize to facilitate the learner's exploring, understanding, and acting upon skill performance during the Summary. If the learner cannot perform to standards at the Summary, then the learner must be recycled through the learning process.

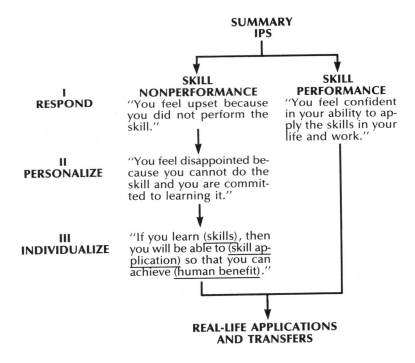

SUMMARY
IPS

	SKILL NONPERFORMANCE	SKILL PERFORMANCE
I RESPOND	"You feel upset because you did not perform the skill."	"You feel confident in your ability to apply the skills in your life and work."
II PERSONALIZE	"You feel disappointed because you cannot do the skill and you are committed to learning it."	
III INDIVIDUALIZE	"If you learn (skills), then you will be able to (skill application) so that you can achieve (human benefit)."	

REAL-LIFE APPLICATIONS
AND TRANSFERS

Interpersonal Processing in the Summary

You may want to practice managing Summary learning in your specialty skills content. Outline your teaching delivery plan for the Summary. Indicate how you will use your management skills to implement your delivery plan learning.

SUMMARY TEACHING DELIVERY PLAN:

_____

_____

_____

_____

_____

LEARNING MANAGEMENT SKILLS:

_____

_____

_____

_____

_____

Practicing LMS in the Summary

Exercising

You now know how to use your learning management skills to implement your teaching delivery plan. You can use your learning management skills to teach any material while "thinking on your feet," in or out of the teaching context. You can apply these skills in any critical situation that involves teaching and learning. For example, you can employ learning management skills for teaching family members, employees, teachers, learners, or trainees to manage their own learning.

SKILL OBJECTIVE:

Learners will manage their own learning by using learning management skills under real-life conditions at a level of effective applications.

TEACHING DELIVERY PLAN:

Content Development, Content Organization, Training Methods.

LEARNING MANAGEMENT SKILLS:

Content Processing, Interpersonal Processing.

Exercising LMS

You may wish to do a repeat exercise using your learning management skills. Apply the learning management skills to a variety of living, learning, or working contexts. Develop and implement your teaching delivery plan for these applications.

SKILL OBJECTIVE:

_____

_____

_____

TEACHING DELIVERY PLAN:

_____

_____

_____

LEARNING MANAGEMENT SKILLS:

_____

_____

_____

Repeating LMS

Describe how you might apply your learning management skills within living, learning, and working settings. Try to identify as many applications as possible.

LIVING: _____

_____

_____

LEARNING: _____

_____

_____

WORKING: _____

_____

_____

Applying LMS

Summarizing

Perhaps you can now outline how you would employ your learning management skills to implement your teaching delivery plan.

You should feel confident if you are able to outline how you plan to implement your teaching delivery plan. A successful outline indicates that we have achieved our training skill objective.

The teachers will make teaching deliveries by implementing learning management skills under formal and informal conditions at levels that facilitate their learners' skill performances.

Indexing LMS

You should feel very pleased with your learning management skills if you are able to manage the learners' learning. Again, your learning management skills emphasize using your CPS and IPS simultaneously in conjunction with each other.

TEACHING DELIVERY PLANS:

> Content Development, Content
> Organization, Teaching Methods

LEARNING MANAGEMENT SKILLS:

> **CONTENT** Diagnosing, Goal-Setting
> **PROCESSING** Programming
> **SKILLS:**
>
> **INTERPERSONAL** Responding, Personalizing,
> **PROCESSING** Individualizing
> **SKILLS:**

CONTENT ORGANIZATION

TEACHING METHODS	Review CS	Overview SA	Present SS	Exercise SS	Summarize SP
TELL	CPS	CPS	CPS	CPS	CPS
	&	&	&	&	&
SHOW	IPS	IPS	IPS	IPS	IPS
	L	T & L	T & L	L	L
DO					

Summarizing LMS

Managing the learners' learning is the heart of the teaching delivery. It means that the teacher has responded to the learners' frames of reference from both the external frame of reference of the content and the internal frames of reference of the learners. Learning management means that the teacher has "hooked up" the teaching content and the learners in the ultimate outcome of learning and development: the teacher has built the learning experience around the recipients of the experience, the learners who are going to go out and apply and transfer these skills to tasks in their real-life, world-of-work environment.

186

References

Aspy, D. N. *Toward a Technology for Humanizing Education.* Champaign, IL. Research Press, 1972.

Aspy, D. N., and Roebuck, F. N. *KIDS Don't Learn from People They Don't Like.* Amherst, MA.: Human Resource Development Press, 1977.

Berenson, D. H., Berenson, S. R., and Carkhuff, R. R. *The Skills of Teaching —Lesson Planning Skills.* Amherst, MA.: Human Resource Development Press, 1978.

Berenson, S. R., Berenson, D. H., and Carkhuff, R. R. *The Skills of Teaching—Teaching Delivery Skills.* Amherst, MA.: Human Resource Development Press, 1979.

Berliner, D. C. *Instructional Time in Research on Teaching.* San Francisco: Far West Laboratory for Educational Research and Development, 1977.

Bloom, B. S., Englehart, M. D., Furst, E. J., Hill, W. H., and Krathwohl, D. R. *A Taxonomy of Educational Objectives: Handbook I, The Cognitive Domain.* NY: Longmans, Green, 1956.

Carkhuff, R. R. *Helping and Human Relations. Volumes I and II.* New York: Holt, Rinehart & Winston, 1969.

Carkhuff, R. R. *The Development of Human Resources.* NY: Holt, Rinehart & Winston, 1969.

Carkhuff, R. R. *The Art of Helping.* Amherst, MA: Human Resource Development Press, 1983.

Carkhuff, R. R., and Berenson, D. H. *The Skilled Teacher.* Amherst, MA: Human Resource Development Press, 1981.

Carkhuff, R. R., Berenson, D. H., and Pierce, R. M. *The Skills of Teaching—Interpersonal Skills.* Amherst, MA: Human Resource Development Press, 1977.

Clark, D. C. "Teaching Concepts in the Classroom." *Journal of Education Psychology,* 1971, *62,* 253–278.

Flanders, N. A. "Diagnosing and Utilizing Social Structures in Classroom Learning." In *The Dynamics of Instructional Groups,* National Society for the Study of Education, 59th Yearbook, Part II. Chicago: University of Chicago Press, 1960.

Flanders, N. A. "Teacher Influence in the Classroom: Research on Classroom Climate." In *Theory and Research in Teaching.* Edited by A. Bellack. NY: Columbia Teacher's College, 1963.

Flanders, N. A. *Analyzing Teaching Behavior.* Reading, MA: Addison-Wesley, 1970.

French, W., and Associates. *Behavioral Goals of General Education in High School.* NY: Russell Sage Foundation, 1957.

Gage, N. L., ed. *The Psychology of Teaching Methods.* Chicago: University of Chicago Press, 1976.

Gage, N. L. *The Scientific Basis of the Art of Teaching.* NY: Teachers College Press, 1977.

Hudgins, B. B. *Self-Contained Training Materials for Teacher Education.* Bloomington, Indiana, National Center for the Development of Training Materials in Teacher Education, Indiana University, 1974.

Kaya, E., Gerhard, M., Staslewski, A., and Berenson, D. H. *Developing a Theory of Educational Practices for the Elementary School.* Norwalk, CT: Ford Foundation Fund for the Improvement of Education, 1967.

Kearney, N. C. *Elementary School Objectives.* NY: Russell Sage Foundation, 1953.

Lumsdaine, A. A. "Educational Technology, Programmed Learning and Instructional Science." In *Theories of Learning and Instruction,* National Society for the Study of Education, 63rd Yearbook, Part 1. Chicago: University of Chicago, Press, 1964.

Mager, R. F. *Preparing Instructional Objectives.* San Francisco: Fearon Publishers, 1962.

Pfeiffer, Isobel L. "Teaching in Ability-Grouped English Classes: A Study of Verbal Interaction and Cognitive Goals." *Journal of Teacher Education, 1966, 17,* No.3.

Smith, W. I., and Moore, J. W. "Size of Step and Caring." *Psychological Reports,* 1962, *10,* 287–294.

III.
SUMMARY
AND OVERVIEW

*T*he teaching and learning process culminates in evaluating the learners' achievements. The chapters on teaching and learning achievement are organized around the basic principles of learning as follows:

Chapter 6—Teaching Evaluation Skills
All productive learning is evaluated by process and outcome measurements.
Chapter 7—The Teaching Process
All the productive learning is facilitated by content and teaching skills.

Learner achievement culminates the teaching and learning process.

6.
Teaching Evaluation Skills

For most teachers, evaluation means quantitatively more and qualitatively less paper work. Many teachers see the current emphasis upon standardized testing as an obstacle to teaching and learning. They are more right than wrong because for most purposes standardized testing is unrelated to real-life functioning. Yet rather than retreat from evaluation, these teachers must address it as an integral part of instructional design. We do not know our effects until we have assessed them. We cannot improve teaching until we have evaluated its impact upon learning.

Basically, evaluation procedures ask the question: did we achieve what we said we would achieve? We cannot practice any profession without asking this most fundamental of questions. We must know if what we do is valuable to others and ourselves. We must be shaped by the feedback that we get from our evaluations. Just as we ask the learners to recycle the learning process based upon the feedback they receive, so must we recycle the teaching process based upon the evaluations we receive. The evaluations are calculated to tell us whether we achieve our objectives or not. If not, they allow us to trace back to process the deficits in our teaching approaches.

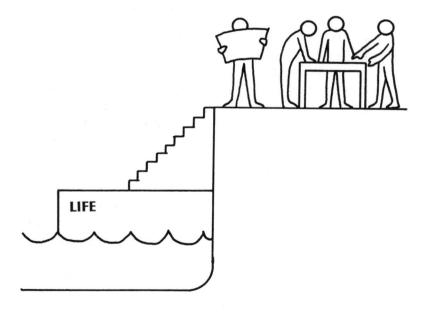

Teaching Evaluation

The most fundamental principle of evaluation is the principle of integrity: if we accomplish our teaching objectives, then we will have fulfilled our constructive intentions so that we remain integral. Systematic evaluations flow from systematic processes (Carkhuff, 1969, 1971, 1983). Non-systematic evaluations are random by-products of non-systematic processes. Thus, productive teachers measure what they attempted to accomplish. While the indices of this measurement should be independent of the process, it is patently absurd to use measures that are totally unrelated to the process. We get what we teach for—no more, no less (Carkhuff and Berenson, 1976). Generalization effects are serendipitous and unreplicable. Thus, our tests and measurements should reflect the process we have implemented to achieve our objectives. Ultimately, we must ask the basic evaluation question: did we or did we not achieve the teaching objective?

Principles of Evaluation

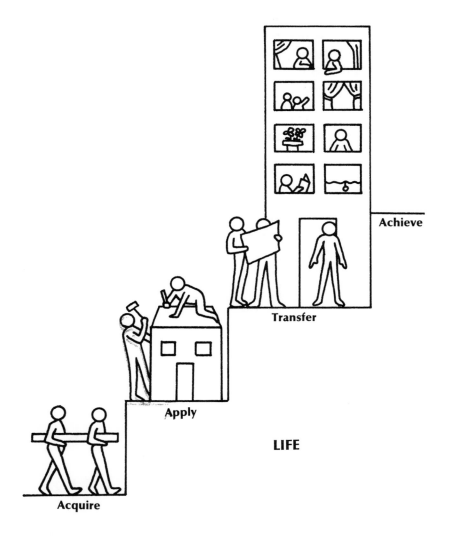

Acquire

Apply

Transfer

Achieve

LIFE

Teaching Evaluation Skills

The teaching objective for this lesson is as follows:

The teachers will evaluate the teaching-learning process by using systematic evaluation skills under formal and informal conditions and at levels that facilitate teacher skill improvement and learner achievement.

Before you learn evaluation skills, you may want an index of your skills in this area. Perhaps you can outline how you would evaluate achievement of objectives in your specialty content. Simply outline the measures of goal achievement you would employ.

_____

_____

_____

_____

_____

Indexing Evaluation

You will be happy if you emphasized simple assessments of goal achievement: did the learners achieve the teaching objective? Shy of this basic question, there are evaluations of task transfers, skill applications, content acquisition and process movement. Together, these measures of process and outcome enable us to trace the movement of the learners toward achieving the teaching objective.

LEVELS OF EVALUATION	INDICES
5 **Goal Achievement:**	Did the learners achieve the goals?
4 **Task Transfers:**	Did the learners transfer the skills to their real-life contextual tasks?
3 **Skill Applications:**	Did the learners apply the skills to the teaching objectives?
2 **Content Acquisition:**	Did the learners acquire the skill content?
1 **Process Movement:**	Did the learners E-U-A- the teaching delivery?

Overviewing Evaluation

Evaluating Process

The essential task in evaluating the learning process is to measure the learners' movements in receiving the skills. The learners' process movements can be measured according to their levels of involving, exploring, understanding, acting, and recycling with the learning experience. Usually, we begin with assessments of their recycling: are the learners involved in an ongoing E-U-A learning process? If so, we move to the next stage of evaluation. If not, we assess their level of acting. We continue in this manner until we have assessed the learners' levels of involvement.

LEVELS OF PROCESS MOVEMENT	INDICES
5 Recycling:	Did the learners recycle the E-U-A learning process in the learning experience?
4 Acting:	Did the learners act to achieve their goals in the learning experience?
3 Understanding:	Did the learners understand their goals with the learning experience?
2 Exploring:	Did the learners explore where they were in relation to the learning experience?
1 Involving:	Did the learners become involved in the process by attending, observing, and listening?

Evaluating Process

For example, we might employ the following indices to assist us in discriminating the levels of learner
process movement in delivering our learning skills content. You already know some sub-indices from your ex-
posure to attending skills. Clearly, it would be helpful
if the learners have been taught what is expected of
them. These learning skills are incorporated in other
materials (Carkhuff, 1984a, 1984b; Carkhuff and Berenson,
1981).

LEVELS OF PROCESS MOVEMENT	INDICES
5 Recycling:	Recycling Acting Recycling Understanding Recycling Exploring
4 Acting:	Implementing Programs Individualizing Programs Developing Programs
3 Understanding:	Defining Goals Personalizing Goals Setting Goals
2 Exploring:	Responding to Selves Diagnosing Selves Analyzing Experience
1 Involving:	Listening Observing Attending Physically

Evaluating Learner Movement

You may find it helpful to evaluate your learners' process movements when you make your teaching delivery. Be sure that your teaching delivery emphasizes all of the teaching skills that facilitate the learners' process movements, i.e., your LMS, IPS, and CPS. That way you can stay attuned to the indices of learner movement. Remember to begin with recycling discrimination and to work your way forward or backward through branching.

LEVELS OF PROCESS MOVEMENT	INDICES
5 Recycling:	_____
	_____
4 Acting:	_____
	_____
3 Understanding:	_____
	_____
2 Exploring:	_____
	_____
1 Involving:	_____
	_____

Exercising Evaluating Process

Evaluating Acquisition

The essential task in evaluating the acquisition of content is to determine the level of skills and knowledge possessed by the learners. These discriminations involve the levels of factual, conceptual, and principle knowledge. They emphasize the level of skill performance, including especially the level of skill steps performed. Usually, the evaluation begins with the skills: can the learners perform the skills? If they can, we move to the next stage of evaluation. If they cannot, we discriminate the level of skill steps the learners can perform. If they have skill step deficits, we discriminate the levels of supportive knowledge they possess.

LEVELS OF ACQUISITION	INDICES
5 **Skill Objective:**	Can the learners perform the skills?
4 **Skill Steps:**	Can the learners perform the skill steps?
3 **Principles:**	Did the learners acquire the principles?
2 **Concepts:**	Did the learners acquire all of the conceptual knowledge?
1 **Facts:**	Did the learners acquire all of the factual knowledge?

Evaluating Acquisition

For example, we might employ the following in-dices to assist us in discriminating the levels of learner acquisition after delivering our learning skills content. You already know all of the definitions that you need to elaborate upon these indices.

LEVELS OF ACQUISITION	INDICES
5 **Skill Objective:**	Operationally defined objectives (i.e., components, functions, processes, conditions, standards).
4 **Skill Steps:**	Steps to be performed (i.e., **Do** steps, sub-steps, and **before, during**, and after **think** steps).
3 **Principles:**	Prepositional clauses defining cause-effect relationships.
2 **Concepts:**	Verbs defining basic activities or functions.
1 **Facts:**	Nouns defining basic ingredients or components.

Evaluating Learner Skills

Again, you may find it helpful to evaluate your learners' content acquisition after you have made your teaching delivery. Be sure to develop indices of skill steps and knowledge as well as the skill objective. Remember to begin with the assessment of the highest level of acquisition, i.e., the objective, and to branch from this discrimination.

LEVELS OF ACQUISITION	INDICES
5 Skill Objective:	_____
	_____
4 Skill Steps:	_____
	_____
3 Principles:	_____
	_____
2 Concepts:	_____
	_____
1 Facts:	_____
	_____

Exercising Evaluating Acquisition

Evaluating Application

The essential task in evaluating skill applications is to determine the level of application to the teaching objective. These discriminations emphasize whether or not the learners applied their skills to the dimensions of the skill objectives: components, functions, processes, conditions, and standards. Usually, we begin with discriminations at the highest levels: whether or not the learners achieved standards of excellence in their application of the skill. We then branch forward to the next stage of evaluation or backward to the previous level of skill application, depending upon the discriminations we make.

LEVELS OF APPLICATION	INDICES
5 **Standards:**	Did the learners apply their skills to the intended levels of excellence?
4 **Conditions:**	Did the learners apply their skills to the basic conditions of objectives?
3 **Processes:**	Did the learners apply their skills to the basic methods of objectives?
2 **Functions:**	Did the learners apply their skills to the basic purposes of objectives?
1 **Components:**	Did the learners apply their skills to the basic ingredients of objectives?

Evaluating Application

For example, we might employ the following indices to assist in discriminating the levels of learner application to learning skills objectives. This should constitute a good review of defining skill objectives.

LEVELS OF APPLICATION	INDICES
5 **Standards:**	How well is it being done?
4 **Conditions:**	Where and when is it being done?
3 **Processes:**	How is it being done?
2 **Functions:**	What is being done?
1 **Components:**	Who and what is involved?

Evaluating Skill Application

Again, you may find it helpful to evaluate your learners' skill applications after they have acquired the content. Be sure you have indices of the dimensions of the skill objective. Remember to begin with the highest level discrimination and to branch from there.

LEVELS OF APPLICATION	INDICES
5 Standards:	_____
	_____
4 Conditions:	_____
	_____
3 Processes:	_____
	_____
2 Functions:	_____
	_____
1 Components:	_____
	_____

Exercising Evaluating Application

Evaluating Transfer

The task in evaluating transfer is directly analogous to that of evaluating application. The difference is that the skill application is planned and the transfer is not planned. Nevertheless, even in a school setting, there are a variety of opportunities for assessing task transfers. Again, we branch from the discriminations of the highest levels of transfer.

LEVELS OF TRANSFER	INDICES
5 **Standards:**	Did the learners transfer their skills to the measures of excellence in task performance?
4 **Conditions:**	Did the learners transfer their skills to basic contexts of tasks?
3 **Processes:**	Did the learners transfer their skills to basic methods of tasks?
2 **Functions:**	Did the learners transfer their skills to basic purposes of tasks?
1 **Components:**	Did the learners transfer their skills to basic ingredients of tasks?

Evaluating Transfer

For example, we might employ the following indices to assist in discriminating the levels of learner transfer to tasks other than the learning skills objectives, i.e., tasks involving peers or other teachers, officials, or parents. Again, we would employ the same essential dimensions of skill objectices.

LEVELS OF TRANSFER	INDICES
5 Standards:	How well?
4 Conditions:	Where and when?
3 Processes:	How?
2 Functions:	What?
1 Components:	Who?

Evaluating Task Transfers

Again, you might find it helpful to evaluate your learners' skill transfers to real-life tasks. Emphasize your dimensions of the skill objective. Begin with the highest level discrimination.

LEVELS OF TRANSFER	INDICES
5 **Standards:**	_____
	_____
4 **Conditions:**	_____
	_____
3 **Processes:**	_____
	_____
2 **Functions:**	_____
	_____
1 **Components:**	_____
	_____

Exercising Evaluating Transfers

Evaluating Achievement

The essential task in evaluating objective achievement is making the basic discrimination: did the learners achieve the original teaching goal? Further refinements on this achievement discriminate levels of productivity in achieving the goal: were the learners efficient and/or effective in achieving the goal or were the learners in-efficient and/or ineffective in achieving the goal. In evaluating levels of achievement, it may be most facili-tative to determine, first, whether or not the goal was achieved (Level 3); second, if so, whether it was achieved efficiently and/or effectively (Levels 4 and 5); if not, whether it was deficit in efficiency and/or effectiveness (Levels 1 and 2).

LEVELS OF ACHIEVEMENT	INDICES
5 Productive:	Were the learners efficient and effective in achieving the goal?
4 Additive:	Were the learners particularly efficient or effective in achieving the goal?
3 Objective:	Did the learners achieve the target goal?
2 Subtractive:	Were the learners inefficient or ineffec-tive in achieving the goal?
1 Non-Productive:	Were the learners inefficient and ineffec-tive in achieving the goal?

Evaluating Achievement

For example, we might employ the following indices to assist in discriminating the levels of learner achievement of the teaching goal of learning computer processing skills in preparation for any career. In other words, we are evaluating whether the human processing (learning skills) facilitated learning computer processing (technical skills). In so doing, we would employ the following indices:

LEVELS OF ACHIEVEMENT	INDICES
5 **Productive:**	Overachieved in results; Before time with minimal resource expenditures.
4 **Additive:**	Overachieved; or Before time with minimal resource expenditures.
3 **Objective:**	Achieved; on time.
2 **Subtractive:**	Underachieved in results; or Late with maximum resource expenditures.
1 **Non-Productive:**	Underachieved in results; Late with maximum resource expenditures.

Evaluating Objective Achievement

Again, you might find it facilitative to evaluate your learners' levels of achievement of your original teaching goals. Begin with discrimination of goal achievement and branch to incremental or decremental levels of productivity.

LEVELS OF ACHIEVEMENT	INDICES
5 Productive:	_____
	_____
4 Additive:	_____
	_____
3 Objective:	_____
	_____
2 Subtractive:	_____
	_____
1 Non-Productive:	_____
	_____

Exercising Evaluating Achievement

Exercising

We can apply the evaluation skills in a variety of living, learning, and working contexts. However, in this regard, it is important to remember that we can assess systematically only those programs that we have designed, developed, and implemented systematically. We can teach our learners to evaluate their own learning programs' process and outcomes: process movement; content acquisition; skill application; task transfers; and goal achievements.

SKILL OBJECTIVE: *Learners will evaluate learning programs by using systematic evaluation procedures in the classroom and at levels that provide them feedback in shaping the learning processes.*

PROCESS: _____

_____

ACQUISITION: _____

_____

APPLICATION: _____

_____

TRANSFER: _____

_____

ACHIEVEMENT: _____

_____

Exercising Evaluation Skills

You may wish to repeat your evaluation skills. Apply the evaluation skills to living and working contexts. Develop your process, acquisition, application, transfer and achievement measures.

SKILL OBJECTIVE: _____

_____

PROCESS: _____

_____

ACQUISITION: _____

_____

APPLICATION: _____

_____

TRANSFER: _____

_____

ACHIEVEMENT: _____

_____

Repeating Evaluation Skills

Try to make a variety of living, learning and working applications with your specialty skill content.

_____

_____

_____

_____

_____

_____

_____

_____

_____

_____

Applying Evaluation Skills

Summarizing

Perhaps you can again take some aspect of your specialty content and outline how you would evaluate its goal achievement. Simply outline the measures of goal achievement you would employ.

_____

_____

_____

_____

If you are able to evaluate your specialty content achievements, then we are confident that you will be able to pursue our evaluation objective throughout your professional career:

The teachers will evaluate the teaching-learning process by using systematic evaluation skills under formal and informal conditions and at levels that facilitate teacher skill improvement and learner achievement.

Indexing Evaluation Skills

Again, we can evaluate systematically only that which we have designed, developed, and implemented systematically. We can see that teaching is initiated with teaching goals. Therefore, teaching must in the final analysis be evaluated by the level of achievement of these goals. Similarly, the other levels of process and outcome are related according to their systematic development and evaluation.

PHASES OF DEVELOPMENT   LEVELS OF EVALUATION

PHASES OF DEVELOPMENT	LEVELS OF EVALUATION
Goals Established ↓	5 Goal Achievement
Task Analyzed ↓	4 Task Transfers
Skills Objectified ↓	3 Skill Applications
Content Developed ↓	2 Content Acquisition
Process Delivered	1 Process Movement

Summarizing Evaluation Skills

In the end, we either achieve our objective or we do not. The pursuit of the objectives is what shapes our integrity. When we learn to achieve our objectives with maximum efficiency and effectiveness, then we may say that we are productive in that specific area. We may recycle our efforts in other areas. As we are shaped by our evaluations, we move increasingly toward becoming more and more productive: using minimal resources to achieve maximum results. We build our integrity, pure and directionful, cell-by-cell in this manner. Increasingly, we develop an x-ray vision that enables us to see things in sharp relief. Always, we elevate our visions of the ideals to be accomplished as we face and answer the basic anxieties of human existence: are we good enough?

References

Carkhuff, R. R. *Helping and Human Relations.* New York, NY: Holt, Rinehart & Winston, 1969.

Carkhuff, R. R. *The Development of Human Resources.* New York, NY: Holt, Rinehart & Winston, 1971.

Carkhuff, R. R. *Sources of Human Productivity.* Amherst, MA: Human Resource Development Press, 1983.

Carkhuff, R. R. *Human Processing and Human Productivity.* Amherst, MA: Carkhuff Institute of Human Technology, in press, 1984(a).

Carkhuff, R. R. *Productivity Processing.* Amherst, MA: Carkhuff Institute of Human Technology, in press, 1984(b).

Carkhuff, R. R. and Berenson, B. G. *Teaching As Treatment.* Amherst, MA: Human Resource Development Press, 1976.

Carkhuff, R. R. and Berenson, D. H. *The Skills of Learning.* Amherst, MA: Carkhuff Institute of Human Technology, 1981.

7. The Teaching Process

The currency of the future will be ideas in the human mind, not dollars in the pocket. When teachers negotiate to improve their own learning opportunities as well as the teaching and learning environment, then they will begin to integrate and embody the systems and skills of the Age of Information. The American dream of freedom of choice and opportunity to improve is alive and well. Productive teachers who deliver the skills to learners will be respected as the sources of the dreams and will be paid as the indispensible contributors they are.

The ultimate test of teaching is learning. The skills of teaching facilitate the skills of learning. Teaching achievement is reflected in the learners' achievements. All of these statements reflect the critical nature of the role of the teacher as the facilitator of learning.

Productive learning takes place when learners employ their learning skills to process stimulus input into response outputs (see Figure 7-1): exploring and analyzing the learning experience; understanding and operationalizing the learning goals; acting and technologizing the learning programs (Carkhuff, 1983). Productive teaching takes place when the teachers employ their teaching skills to facilitate learner processing: content processing skills; interpersonal processing skills; and learning management skills.

All of these and learning skills are involved in preparing and making a teaching delivery (see Figure 7-2). In the teaching diamond, we see that the teachers use their content preparation skills to prepare the content and develop their learning management plan for the learners. The teachers employ their content processing skills (CPS) to deliver the content to the learners. The teachers apply their interpersonal processing skills (IPS) to relate the learners to the content. The simultaneous application of CPS and IPS in implementing the learning management plan constitutes the

PHASES OF LEARNING

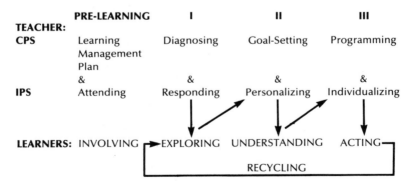

Figure 7-1. Teaching and Learning Process

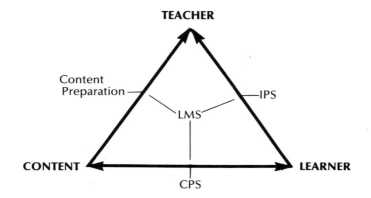

Figure 7-2. The Learning Management Skills Core of the Interactional Teaching Triangle

learning management skills (LMS) core of the interactional teaching triangle.

Instructional System Design

All of these teaching and learning skills are part of a larger intervention system design system (Carkhuff, 1983) (see Figure 7-3). An intervention system is

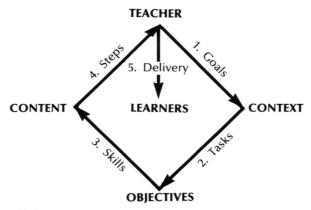

Figure 7-3. The Stations of Intervention System Design

initiated with the establishment of productivity goals based upon individual, organizational, or societal needs (Station 1). The system is implemented with an analysis of the contextual tasks the learners need to perform in order to achieve the productivity goals (Station 2). In turn, the tasks are broken out into the specific skills that comprise them (Station 3). These skills constitute the objectives which initiate the instructional system design (ISD): developing the teaching content and the teaching delivery plan (Station 4); and making and receiving the teaching delivery (Station 5).

For example, organizational productivity and individual performance goals may be established by the school or community board in conjunction with the superintendent and other decision-makers. The organizational productivity may have to do with increasing district learner achievement while reducing resource expenditures. The individual learner performance goals, in turn, may have to do with increasing basic communication or computation skills within a given class in less time.

Transitionally, the tasks needed to achieve the goals are analyzed. These tasks emphasize the processing that transforms the inputs to the outputs needed to achieve the productivity goals. For example, the organizational productivity goals of increasing learner achievement may emphasize developing teaching staff delivery task performance. The individual learner performance goals, in turn, may emphasize learning—how-to-learn—whether reading, writing or math.

After the productivity goals have been established and the contextual tasks have been analyzed, the teaching objectives are defined. It is at this point that productive teachers initiate their use of their ISD skills. They define the teaching objectives in terms of what is to be done and how to do it. For example, the learning-to-learn skills may be defined in terms of analyzing, operationalizing and technologizing skills.

Following the definition of skill objectives, the productive teachers employ ISD skills to develop the teaching content in terms of skill steps and supportive knowledge. For example, the learning-to-learn skills content may include such skill steps as learner analysis of the components, functions, and processes of a learning experience.

Armed with the skills content, the productive teachers employ ISD skills to organize the content and methods for presentation. For example, in the case of the learning content, the orderly principles of organizing content must be employed: learner reviewing of contingency skill performance; teacher and learner overview skill applications; teacher presenting and learner exercising skill steps; and learner summarizing skill performance.

Thus, the productive teachers prepare themselves for making their teaching deliveries by using their ISD skills. Again, they make their teaching deliveries by using their teaching delivery skills (TDS): content processing skills (CPS); interpersonal processing skills (IPS); and learning management skills (LMS). In turn, the learners receive the teaching deliveries by using their learning skills (Carkhuff and Berenson, 1984).

Learning achievement is assessed in a counterclockwise manner reflecting the ISD design (see Figure 7-4). The effects of the teaching delivery are assessed in terms of the learning process movement of the learners (Station 6). In turn, the learners' levels of content acquisition (Station 7) and the learners' levels of application to the skill objective (Station 8) are assessed. Finally, the transfers to the real-life contextual tasks (Station 9) and the levels of productivity achievement (Station 10) are assessed.

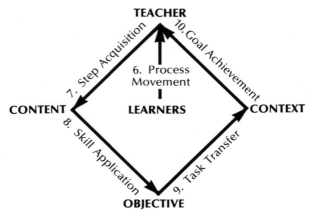

Figure 7-4. The Stations of Evaluation of Intervention Systems Design

Teaching as Instructional Design

These ISD skills become particularly important in the Age of Information when data inputs are constantly changing (Carkhuff, 1983). They require that the teachers constantly change the instructional design. No longer can the teacher rely upon learning and delivering a relatively stable content. Indeed, the productive teacher of the Information Age will involve the learners in instructional design.

The educational changes brought about by the Information Age are vast and profound (Carkhuff, 1983, 1984). The most critical of these shifts is reflected in the emergence of human and information resource development as the critical sources of economic growth. Whereas capital and natural resources once dominated economic growth, human and natural resources now account for nearly all of productivity growth. Thus, the quality of personnel and their configurations in industry along with advancements in knowledge now account for more than 80% of productivity growth. Indeed, these dimensions can be seen most clearly in circular interaction with each other: developing human resources contributes to developing information resources; developing information resources contributes directly to developing human resources.

In this context, education is the critical source of human and information resource development. It accounts for more than 80% of human and information resource development. Thus, by teaching humans the processing skills needed to produce advancements in knowledge and by using the advancements in knowledge to produce more productive human resources, productive teachers become the central players in a great new Age of Productivity (Carkhuff, 1983, 1984).

Nowhere is the emphasis upon productivity felt more highly than in education. Sometimes teachers are frustrated because they feel like they are being asked to make something out of nothing. Yet the personal resources they have to fall back upon are enormous: teachers are energized by their reinvigorated fitness, catalyzed by their unbounded commitment to contribute to future generations and technologized by their sharpened skills in their specialty content and teaching and learning.

The future of a nation may be found in the minds and skills of its children. The vision of the future may be found in the minds and skills of their teachers.

References

Carkhuff, R. R. *Sources of Human Productivity.* Amherst, MA: Human Resources Development Press, 1983.

Carkhuff, R. R. *The EXEMPLAR: The Exemplary Performer in the Age of Productivity.* Amherst, MA: Human Resource Development Press, 1984.

Carkhuff, R. R. and Berenson, D. H. *The Skills of Learning.* Amherst, MA: Human Resource Development Press, in press, 1984.

Author Index

Subject Index